W9-BVG-891

AAHE-ERIC/Higher Education Research Report No. 8, 1980

Student Retention Strategies

Oscar T. Lenning
Ken Sauer
Philip E. Beal

Theodore Lownik Library
Illinois Benedictine College
Lisle, Illinois 60532

Prepared by

ERIC ®

Clearinghouse on Higher Education
The George Washington University

Published by

AAHE

American Association for Higher Education

LC78
148
L46
1980

WITHDRAWN

ERIC® **Clearinghouse on Higher Education**
One Dupont Circle, Suite 630
Washington, D.C. 20036

American Association for Higher Education
One Dupont Circle, Suite 780
Washington, D.C. 20036

This publication was prepared with funding from the National Institute of Education, U.S. Department of Education, under contract no. 400-77-0073. The opinions expressed in this report do not necessarily reflect the positions or policies of NIE or the Department.

Foreword

Few organizations, whether profit or non-profit, service or product oriented, have failed to the degree that higher education institutions have in recognizing that part of their survival is dependent on retaining current customers or clients. The business adage that "what every company wants to do is to produce a product that costs a dime to make, a dollar to sell, and that is habit forming," exemplifies the concept that organizational success depends on maintaining current customers and encouraging returning business. At times it seemed that, once students were accepted, an institution made no conscious effort to help them complete their program.

During the '60s and the early '70s there were two primary reasons why an institution had limited concern with the retention of its students. The first was that it had more students than its faculty or facilities could handle. If a number of students did not continue to enroll, it was not a problem since many other students were waiting to take their place. The second reason involved a philosophical interpretation of equal education opportunity and the maintaining of academic standards. Many felt that they fulfilled their obligations for equal educational opportunity if students had easy access to the institutions. There was also an assumption that academic standards would suffer if special considerations were given to any particular group of students, and therefore all were judged by the same criteria. As a result it was not unusual to have more than a 50 percent dropout rate before graduation.

As higher education enters the '80s these two conditions have changed. The growth in enrollment has stopped and the 18 to 24 year old student cohort is predicted to decrease 25 percent by the mid-1990s. Institutions now or will have a need to insure a steady student enrollment. Concurrently, there has been a change in the attitude towards what achieving the goal of equal educational opportunity actually entails. Access to higher education is no longer sufficient. Institutions are increasingly giving special attention to the educationally, financially, and physically disadvantaged in an effort to make their chances for academic success more equal to those who are more fortunate. The importance of developing strategies that will help retain students now has become obvious.

The predicted results of greater attention to retaining students are many. The primary one is that institutions will have to attract 20 percent fewer new students to maintain their enrollments if they take better care that their current students do not leave the institution before completion of their program. Other predicted benefits of retention strategies are that student morale will increase, that student, faculty, and institutional interaction will become more positive, and that alumni relations will be more supportive.

Acknowledging that it is critical for an institution to have a successful retention program is one thing; accomplishing this is quite another. In this Research Report, Oscar T. Lenning and Kenneth Sauer, senior staff associates with the National Center for Higher Education Management Systems (NCHEMS), and Philip E. Beal, a former visiting scholar at NCHEMS and currently dean of students at Saganaw Valley State College, have conducted a thorough review of the major student retention strategies developed by institutions. In this review, they identify different types of retention strategies, review the various activities within these strategies and propose criteria and recommendations that institutions will find profitable as they develop their own retention programs.

Jonathan D. Fife
Director
ERIC® Clearinghouse on Higher Education

Acknowledgement

Acknowledgement and appreciation are hereby expressed to Dr. Robert Cope for reviewing the manuscript and providing helpful suggestions.

Contents

Overview 1

Types of Retention and Their Empirical Correlates 6
Types of retention 6
Correlates of retention 10

Action Strategies to Improve Retention 17
The WWISR study 17
Single-facet retention approaches 18
Multifaceted approaches to improving retention 40

Conclusion 46

Bibliography 50

Overview

The immediate historical impetus for this study derives from a project funded by the National Institute of Education that began in the fall of 1977. That project, which built upon previous work done at the National Center for Higher Education Management Systems (NCHEMS) in the areas of educational outcomes and retention/attrition, eventually resulted in the NCHEMS publication *Retention and Attrition: Evidence for Action and Research* (Lenning, Beal, and Sauer 1980). Another project, conducted jointly by NCHEMS and the American College Testing program (ACT) beginning in the fall of 1978, resulted in the joint ACT-NCHEMS publication *What Works in Student Retention?* (Beal and Noel 1980). The present monograph synthesizes the results of the previous studies and integrates new material gathered through the summer of 1980.

The focus of this study is to review the research literature from the standpoint of what strategies are likely to be most effective in retaining students. In some cases the research literature only implies what may be an effective retention strategy, but in other cases observations and results are provided for special action programs that have been designed to keep students in college. In both instances, the purposes of our review is to highlight those research efforts that offer helpful suggestions on how a campus might deal effectively with the problem of retention.

That increasing attention is being placed on retention efforts is evident from the large number of studies on this subject published in recent years. We expect this trend to continue, a judgment that is shared by the widely quoted final report of the Carnegie Council on Policy Studies in Higher Education, *Three Thousand Futures: The Next Twenty Years for Higher Education*. The chapter on enrollments begins with the statement that:

> The most dramatic feature of the next 20 years, as far as we now know, is the prospect of declining enrollments after more than three centuries of fairly steady increase.... Points of enrollment acceleration in history have been 1870 with the increase of growth after the Civil War and following the introduction of the land-grant college movement; 1945 with the G.I. Bill of Rights; and 1960 with the "tidal wave" of students following the high birthrates after World War II. Now there is a deceleration point, with the abrupt and substantial demographic decline in the numbers of young persons. Two points of change, with movements in opposite directions, will have

occurred within one 20-year period. This has never happened before in American history (Carnegie Council 1980, p. 32).

In light of the prospect of declining enrollments, the following judgments of the Carnegie Council appear to be soundly based and not totally surprising:

> We expect colleges to exert an all-out effort to increase the retention rate. We estimate that these efforts may add a 20 percent gain in time spent in college by those who in the past have not completed their four-year degrees and by academic transfer students enrolled in community colleges. Private colleges, in particular, have a great incentive to increase the number of their alumni with degrees since financial support comes proportionately more from them than from those who drop out. We note, however, that the recent retention experience in community colleges has been disappointing and so also have been the transfer rate to four-year colleges. Nevertheless, the internal market of students already on campus is both large and readily available for retention effort (Carnegie Council 1980, pp. 43-44).

Clarity of terminology is important and is reviewed in this document. In brief, student retention means student persistence:

- persistence to the completion of a degree or certificate
- persistence to the completion of a chosen program but short of a degree or certificate
- persistence to completion of a term or a course
- persistence to the attainment of a personal goal but short of a degree or a certificate.

Two kinds of retention studies are reviewed in this monograph. The first is aimed at uncovering the characteristics and attitudes that are common among students who persist and among those who drop out. This type of study is most common and has identified a number of features that distinguish the persister from the nonpersister. These features include:

- high academic performance in high school and first year of college
- familial aspiration for college
- advanced educational level of parents
- high personal educational aspirations
- involvement of the student with the college
- intention to remain to graduation
- perception of financial capacity to pay expenses
- receipt of scholarships, grants, and/or part-time employment on campus
- high prestige and cost of institution

- religious affiliation of institution
- on-campus living
- high-quality and utilization of student support services, especially learning assistance opportunities, advising, and involvement opportunities, both academic and nonacademic
- high-quality and frequent student-faculty interaction
- student-institution fit, including moral and social integration, perceived responsiveness of the institution to students' needs, and the congruence between expectations and opportunities for their realization.

The second kind of retention study focuses on the practical application of retention strategies and their effectiveness in improving retention. This document reviews a number of these studies, beginning with the "What Works in Student Retention?" study (WWISR), the first comprehensive, national survey of action programs designed to improve retention. The action literature is discussed under two major headings: single-facet retention approaches and multifaceted approaches to improving retention.

Twelve kinds of single-facet retention approaches are identified, and their effects on student retention are summarized:

1. *Admissions and recruiting.* When students receive adequate and accurate information from a college, they will be more likely to choose the institution that best meets their needs, which, in turn, will increase their chances of persisting.

2. *Advising.* Improved academic advising is an action program for improving retention that has been implemented by many institutions and, in most cases, is found to contribute to retention.

3. *Counseling.* Counseling has served as a foundation for numerous retention programs with positive results.

4. *Early warning and prediction.* Prediction of potential dropouts can be productive and when combined with one or several early warning strategies can reduce attrition.

5. *Exit interviews.* Even though their observed impact on retention is lower than most other intervention strategies, exit interviews can gather significant information on why students leave and how the institution might change to improve the retention for other students. In addition, a few individuals may remain in the institution as a result of assistance gained through an exit interview.

6. *Extracurricular activities.* The literature indicates that more often than not meaningful participation in extracurricular activities contributes to student retention.

7. *Faculty, staff, and curricular development.* The frequency and quality of faculty and student interactions can contribute

positively to student retention, and in-service faculty/staff development efforts can contribute more favorable student/faculty interaction. Changes in curricular design and emphasis also can be productive.

8. *Financial aid.* Assisting students to cope with their financial problems can contribute to retention as can specific types of aid given to students including scholarships, grants, and on-campus part-time employment.

9. *Housing.* Many studies have demonstrated that on-campus housing including residence halls, fraternities, and sororities improve students' chances of retention.

10. *Learning and academic support.* Learning and academic support services are shown clearly in the literature to have a positive effect on student retention.

11. *Orientation.* Significant improvements in retention rates have been found by institutions that focus on orientation as a retention strategy.

12. *Policy change.* Colleges that redesign policies and procedures for the purpose of improving student retention show significant improvement in their retention rates.

Multifaceted approaches to student retention, where everyone on campus participates in some manner, can be even more effective in improving retention rates than focusing on a single approach. The literature supports attempts by colleges that would combine different programs to improve retention. Several programs working together could have a symbiotic effect and result in increased effectiveness and retention.

For all the types of retention programs referred to above, there also have been cases of failing to significantly influence student retention. Therefore, how the program is carried out (process), and the way that faculty, staff, and students are prepared for and involved in the program, are crucial factors. Furthermore, the specifics that are effective at one institution may not be effective at another. The relationships among and interactions between institutional, faculty and staff, student, and action program characteristics are determining factors. The particular program called for depends on an analysis of attitudes, relationships, faculty and staff capabilities and readiness, student groupings, student needs, projected alternative cost/benefit feasibility, etc. It is clearly an individual institution decision, although knowing what has worked in other institutions and under what conditions can be helpful. An experimental tryout of the tailored approach with small numbers of students may be called for before large-scale implementation is attempted.

The second chapter of this mongraph discusses research studies that imply or suggest relevant retention strategies. The literature is discussed under three major headings: student correlates of retention, institutional correlates of retention, and student institution fit and interaction as correlates of student retention. Chapter three reviews the literature and action programs expressly designed to improve student retention in light of the findings summarized in chapter two. Both chapters expand upon the conclusions reported above and discuss process considerations. Chapter four concludes this monograph with a summary of findings and an assessment of the state-of-the-art in retention research.

Types of Retention and Their Empirical Correlates

College educators increasingly recognize that there is more than one type of student retention and that research findings about retention become more meaningful when this fact is kept in mind. Furthermore, educators recognize that retention rates may vary significantly when student and institutional characteristics are taken into consideration.

Types of retention

Webster's Third New International Dictionary defines retention as "retaining or holding fixed in some place, position, or condition." This definition suggests that from the perspective of the college or university, student retention means keeping students enrolled until they complete their degree or certificate program. As used here, student retention is analogous to the term "student persistence" and is the converse of "student attrition." However, the research literature reveals two additional ways in which retention may be defined: as course or term completion and as personal goal attainment.

Program completion as retention. In the research literature, graduation—the attainment of a diploma or degree—has been the traditional criterion for measuring student retention. Rates usually are computed on the basis of a standard program length for each degree or diploma, such as two years for an associate's degree and four or five years for a bachelor's degree. However, students increasingly are not graduating in the designated *time* period; they are frequently "stopping out" in either a planned or an unplanned interruption of schooling. A second dimension concerning graduation as retention, in addition to time, is *institution;* did the students graduate from their institutions of original entry, or did they graduate elsewhere? A third dimension is whether the students graduated in the *program* they initially entered, for example, engineering or nursing. Interrelating the three dimensions (time, institution, and program) provides six separate definitions of program completion, plus additional combinations. The six separate definitions are as follows:

1. Graduating in the time designated for the degrees or certificates offered
2. Graduating after the time designated for the degrees or certificates offered

3. Graduating at the institution of initial entry
4. Graduating from an institution other than the one in which initially enrolled
5. Graduating in the curricular program initially entered
6. Graduating in a curricular program other than the one in which initially entered

The first two of the above definitions (percentage rates for each could be considered a measure of that type of retention) are defined according to time, the next two according to institution, and the final two according to program completed.

The percentage of all students who graduate from a bachelor's program at the college of initial entry within the designated four or five years has approximated 40 percent over all types of institutions for the last half century, according to Cope and Hannah (1975). As reported by Pantages and Creedon (1978), the typical retention percentage reported across baccalaureate institutions increases from 40 percent when definitions 1 and 3 are combined; to 50 percent for definitions 1, 2, and 3 combined; to 70 percent for definitions 1, 2, 3, and 4 combined. For this last combined definition, El-Khawas and Bisconti (1974) found a graduation rate of 77 percent after ten years for their national sample.

In a national study by Beal and Noel (1980), the average of graduation rates for *five years* after entrance to baccalaureate institutions varied from 53 percent at four-year public institutions to 63 percent at four-year, private secular institutions. Beal and Noel also reported that for two-year colleges the average of graduation rates for *three years* after entry was 61 percent for private institutions and 42 percent for public. Furthermore, within each type of institution the retention percentages can vary greatly. For example, in his review of 35 studies, Summerskill (1962) found institutional retention rates varying from 18 percent to 88 percent.

A study by Martin (1974) demonstrates the importance of definitions 2 and 4. At the end of the 1973 fall quarter at Roane State Community College in Tennessee, 25 percent of those who had been enrolled did not reenroll for the winter quarter. However, when those who transferred to other schools and those who planned to reenroll were deleted from the dropout group, the dropout rate was only 5 percent.

Although Astin's study (1975a, 1975c) of the Cooperative Institutional Research Program (CIRP) national samples of freshmen entering two- and four-year institutions focused only on those who graduated with a bachelor's degree four years after first matriculating, his data illustrate the need to distinguish among the various ways retention can be measured. Astin found that, of those freshmen who had no degree aspiration when they first entered a two-

or four-year institution, 36 percent received a bachelor's degree four years later. While this retention rate is low compared with the retention rate of those freshmen who aspired to a bachelor's degree, master's degree, or doctorate—45 percent, 58 percent, and 62 percent, respectively—it may, in fact, be high considering that this group of students started with no degree aspirations. Similarly, the fact that 13 percent of those freshmen who originally aspired to an associate's degree went on to attain a bachelor's degree may indicate a relatively high retention rate, given the original program completion goals of the students. As these data illustrate, the interpretation of retention rates, as measured by program completion rates, should consider the nature of the student sample.

Astin eliminated from his main study all who aspired to less than a bachelor's degree because he was focusing on baccalaureate graduates. Although such a procedure is endorsed here, the effect of student degree aspiration on retention cannot be controlled completely because students' aspirations change during college attendance.

The student attrition manual developed by the Council for the Advancement of Small Colleges (1978) provides formats for, and illustrates the usefulness of, reporting graduation percentages separately for entering freshmen of a particular year and students transferring in during a particular year, as well as retention percentages at the end of the freshman, sophomore, and junior years of college. Similar formats could be developed for retention percentages according to entering college goal, sex, background characteristics, and time of completion.

It is becoming increasingly accepted among educators that retention should not always be measured by the attainment of a certificate or degree. Some students become "official" attrition statistics because they do not earn a degree or certificate, even though they successfully design and complete informal program objectives of their own.

Course or term completion as retention. Kohen (1978), along with many other researchers, found that dropout rates vary by year in school and that the largest percentage of drop usually takes place during the freshman year, generally before the start of the second term.* Furthermore, the reasons given by the dropouts for leav-

---

*An exception is reported by Newlon and Gaither (1980) who found that a smaller percentage of junior transfers at California State University, Northridge persist during the first semester than is true of freshman during their first semester. Newlon and Gaither also found that most of the transfer students had enrolled after graduation from California community colleges.

ing college and the characteristics of the dropouts tended to vary with the year when the students left school.

Early studies (Iffert 1957; Barger and Hall 1964) found that the final withdrawal decision usually occurs during vacation or other times when the college or university is not in session. Furthermore, Iffert found that more students dropped out at institutions with quarter systems than at institutions with semester systems, possibly because of the "increase in the number of stopping places" (p. 160) or the more time-constraining pressure in a quarter system. A large number of students drop out *during* the term, however; Johnston (1971), for example, reports an average of 17 percent for community colleges.

Sexton's (1965) review of the literature concluded that students tend to drop out more often at the beginning or end of a term than in the middle. Both Sexton and Barger and Hall (1964) found that "early-term withdrawers" gave different reasons for withdrawal than did "late-term withdrawers." Barger and Hall also found that the second group carried a lighter academic load than did the first.

Students who drop out after completing terms or individual courses frequently do so for positive reasons, such as accepting a job after acquiring needed skills through their coursework. Moreover, these students are more likely to return to college at some later time. However, students who drop out during a term often have a more basic disenchantment with postsecondary education. For these students particularly, the "course or term completion" measure of retention probably is more pertinent than the "program completion" measure, especially where the collection and study of withdrawal and retention statistics is for the purpose of improving problem-related retention. Yet, most retention and attrition research has focused on "program completion" retention.

Personal goal attainment as retention. As implied earlier, for some students attendance at college to achieve a personal goal may be more important than completion of certificate or degree requirements. Examples of these personal goals are: developing a particular skill, obtaining a secure job in the area of training, and finding a spouse.

Leaving school for a secure job in their area of training is especially prevalent for career and occupational/technical program students at two-year community colleges. Community college students are enrolled for many reasons other than obtaining a certificate or degree—to obtain a personally desired skill or area of knowledge, to up-grade skills and knowledge, to enrich personal life, to take advantage of an employer-paid educational program, etc. Therefore, it should not be surprising that community college administrators are concerned when legislators or others compare their graduation rates unfavorably with those at other types of colleges.

In light of this, a "personal goal attainment" measure of student retention is entirely legitimate. It is needed especially at community colleges, but also at four-year colleges and universities of all types. It emphasizes the important fact that withdrawal or transfer prior to graduation is not necessarily bad, but can be a positive and desirable step for the student that should be supported and facilitated by the institution. Furthermore, as Haagen (1977) makes clear, in many cases withdrawal may be desirable and positive even when personal goals related to attending college have not been attained. Timmons (1978) found that withdrawal may be a positive step toward forming an identity, establishing one's own priorities, and meeting developmental needs such as independence from parents and self-responsibility.

Although little of the literature addresses this concept of student retention, a study by Nickens (1976) examined attrition at 15 Florida two-year community colleges in relation to the students' educational objectives and their plans to reach them. Many students classified as dropouts stated that they planned to return to college later, but others had entered with plans to take only one or more courses and were satisfied with their goal attainment. Nickens concluded that only 2 percent of the students were legitimate dropouts. Although this may be a limited study, it emphasizes the importance of linking retention and withdrawal to student goals and objectives. Furthermore, with the questioning of the value of a college degree that became common in the early 1970s, enrollment for personal goals is undoubtedly an increasing phenomenon. This trend may be beneficial for higher education but needs to be better understood by institutions.

Correlates of retention

As indicated in the preceding section, almost all research thus far has focused on retention as measured by graduation or lack of graduation and the time that graduation or dropout occurs. Logically, however, it makes sense that course or term completion and personal goal attainment will, for the most part, be correlated with or affected by the same factors, circumstances, and programs. The validity of this assumption needs to be tested empirically, but enough fragmentary evidence exists to suggest that this assumption is correct. Accordingly, this assumption will be held throughout this section and the following chapter on approaches for improving retention. We will be talking about retention in general, and the readers will have to decide for themselves whether to consider only graduation and program completion as retention, or whether to include other types of retention as well.

Lenning, Beal, and Sauer (1980) discussed in depth what the research results suggest as to correlates of retention; here we will summarize the most salient generalizations.

Student correlates of retention. Most research on retention has examined student-report reasons for dropping out, although some research has correlated student characteristics to persistence-withdrawal status. A complex array of student factors is clearly involved in retention and attrition, and the pattern of factors varies with the institution, the instructional program, and the individual.

High school and first-year college grades, the academic rating of the high school attended, and the student's study skills and habits and academic aptitude have been found to have a positive relationship to student retention. Although the demographic characteristics of age and sex are related to the reasons students give for dropping out, they seem to be generally unrelated to the actual dropout rate. In other words, while men and women and older and younger students drop out for different reasons, they tend to drop out with about the same frequency. However, at least two recent studies suggest contrary results: Brigman and Stager (1980) found at Indiana University that males were overrepresented among stopouts and females were overrepresented among dropouts, and Greer (1980) found at a junior college that age was inversely related to persistence in regular programs and directly related to persistence in developmental programs. But when other variables such as socioeconomic level and motivation are controlled, age and sex have not been found to be major factors in retention.

Some relationship does exist for ethnic minority status. Spanish-speaking students tend to drop out more frequently irrespective of other control variables, and Asian and Jewish students consistently tend to drop out less frequently. Blacks and American Indian students generally are found to drop out more frequently only when appropriate other factors are not controlled.

Familial aspirations for college, educational level of parents, personal aspirations for education, and commitment to and involvement of the student and/or family with the college often are positively related to retention. Peng and Fetters (1977), as well as other studies, have concluded that the reason socioeconomic level relates to student retention is because it affects pre-college environment and personality and they, in turn, affect student motivation and aspirations, and not because students cannot afford college. Self-confidence and self-concept are also clearly part of the picture. The specificity of a student's vocational and occupational goals consistently has been found positively related to student retention only in technological and vocational programs. As in the case of high school and home town size where higher retention has been found for students from private high schools and larger high schools in large communities, it is believed that student-institution fit is important, rather than the factors themselves.

Although Pantages and Creedon (1978) concluded that aspirations and motivations and commitment to goals had not been shown to have positive relationships to retention, Lenning, Beal, and Sauer (1980) found otherwise. (Such a relationship is especially clear in a national study by Peng and Fetters [1977] and a single-institution study by Bean [1980] that Pantages and Creedon did not review.) As suggested earlier concerning vocational and occupational goals, however, it is not always a straightforward relationship: other factors such as student-institution fit intervene. Where student-institution fit is poor, commitment to the college and to getting a degree becomes crucial for retention to occur. If students are satisfied with the college and their selection of program, that satisfaction undoubtedly contributes to retention, assuming other factors are not involved. However, retention often may be related as much to a willingness and ability to endure dissatisfaction as to the dissatisfaction itself (Iffert 1957; Michelin 1977). Thus, prestigious private institutions generally have much higher retention rates than other schools, although the reason is not necessarily because of higher satisfaction. Students probably often have more to lose in terms of self-image, emotional commitment, and future career success by dropping out of such institutions. Also, as would be expected, the intention at the time of entrance to school or to a term to transfer or drop out of the college is inversely related to persistance. This intention may be desirable if students have valid reason for it. Conversely, the strong expression of an intention to persist is positively related to retention and may be a best single indicator of retention propensity (Johnson and Chapman 1980).

Concerning financial factors, the student's perception of ability to pay for college may be more important than the student's or family's actual financial situation. Some students with adequate financial support express a concern about finances and withdraw to solve the perceived problem. Other lower-income students with high motivation to persist do not perceive finances as a problem. Finances is the reason most often given by students for withdrawing, but it is also one of the most socially acceptable reasons, and withdrawing students often have to protect their self-image. Fenstemacher (1973) found that withdrawing because of insufficient finances was at least partly the result of students' reluctance to apply for financial aid.

As suggested by this discussion of finances, important underlying reasons for dropping out are not always emphasized by students. For example, experienced interviewers used in studies by Demos (1968), Davis (1970), and Demitroff (1974) perceived different underlying reasons for dropout than had been reported by the students. Davis found that a sizable majority of his community college students blamed the college (bad college experiences, poor college counseling services, and lack of faculty interest), but in-depth counseling sessions revealed that the students actually blamed themselves more than the college.

Astin (1975b, 1975c), in particular, has examined the relationship of different patterns of student financial aid and employment to retention. Although Peng and Fetters' national study (1977) did not find a relationship between scholarships or loans and retention, Astin and others found evidence that, overall, scholarships and grants and part-time employment (particularly on-campus) do contribute to retention. (Astin found the degree of satisfaction with the employment to bear little relationship to retention or attrition.) On the other hand, loans (particularly large ones) and working full time tend to contribute to withdrawal. Working off-campus part time seems to have some positive effect on retention except where the job has been held for a long time and is related to a career opportunity. (Here there may be no real attrition if the personal goal attainment definition of retention is applied.)

Institutional correlates of retention. As mentioned earlier, the prestige of an institution is directly related to its graduation rates, and, for both two-year and four-year colleges, private institutions tend to have higher student retention than do public institutions. In addition, higher-cost institutions tend to have higher retention than lower-cost institutions, and those with a clearly defined mission and role have lower attrition rates than similar institutions with a less well defined mission and role. Colleges with a religious affiliation tend to have greater retention than other colleges, and Roman Catholic colleges tend to have higher retention rates than colleges affiliated with Protestant denominations.

Students living in residence halls tend to have higher retention rates than those living off-campus, whether or not residence hall living is required; and moving from home to a residence hall after the first year tends to improve retention. Fraternity and sorority groups tend to have higher retention rates than students living in residence halls.

The type and quality of student support services also can have a positive relationship to student retention. These support services include counseling; advising; orientation; learning assistance services; extracurricular activities and recreation (if not overdone); participation as tutors, peer counselors, or staff and faculty assistants; and participation in work-study, honors, foreign study, or credit by examination programs.

Astin (1975c) and a number of theorists have posited that strong involvement in academic and social activities is a determiner of student persistance. However, in a study across institutional types, Johnson and Chapman (1980, p. 12) discovered that such involvement "is no guarantee that a student will persist." Having close associations with peers, faculty, or staff is important for student retention. There is also strong evidence (Terenzini and Pascarella 1980a; Pascarella and Terenzini 1980) that both the frequency and quality of faculty-student interaction outside of class are positively related to student retention. In a later study of a specially designed living-learning center at an institution studied earlier, however, Terenzini and Pascarella found that the quality, not the frequency, of the faculty-student interaction was significantly related to student retention (1980b).

Student-institution fit and interactions as correlates of student retention. A number of theories have postualted that what really differentiates persisters from withdrawers is neither student factors nor institutional factors, but rather how the factors interact and fit together (Lenning, Beal, and Sauer 1980, pp. 43-67).* Included among the interactions collectively covered by these theories are moral and social integration, the perceived responsiveness of the institution to the needs students feel, and the congruences between student expectations and the opportunities for those expectations to be realized.

As mentioned earlier, the Pascarella and Terenzini studies demonstrate the importance of the Spady and Tinto formulations, with respect to faculty-student and student-student interactions. Other studies also support these theories: Husband's (1976) work on significant others; Lenning's (1970a, 1970b) research on the effects of discrepancies between student and institutional lifestyles; the Savicki (1970) study relating persistance to interest in

---

*Previously discussed theories include: Tinto's (1975) Social Integration Model; Spady's (1970, 1971) Interaction Model; Holland's (1966, 1973) Personality/Environment Types Theory; Festinger's (1962) Cognitive Dissonance Theory; Alfred's (1974) Symbolic Interaction Model; Cope and Hannah's (1975) Congruence Formulation; Flannery et al. (1973) Society/Student/College Listings; and Starr, Betz, and Menne's (1972) Person/Environment Fit Formulation.

social development; Pervin and Rubin's (1967) examination of discrepancies between self and college, self and other students, and actual college and ideal college; Keniston and Helmreich's (1965) exploration of identity development, frustration tolerances, and parent-student discord; Nasatir's (1969) comparison of student orientation to the dormitory environment in terms of retention; and Heist's (1968) study of able, creative students. There is an abundance of research supporting the Festinger and Holland theories, which relate to our topic, although the research has not focused on student retention as such, and not always on students.

One final interactive theory should be mentioned. Bean (1980) developed a "causal model" of retention, based on the research findings regarding turnover in work organizations and research on student retention, that he summarized as follows:

> ... background characteristics of students must be taken into account in order to understand their interactions within the environment of the institution of higher education .... the student interacts with the institution, perceiving objective measures such as grade point average or belonging to campus organizations, as well as subjective measures such as the practical value of the education and the quality of the institution. These variables are expected to influence the degree to which the student is satisfied with the institution of higher education. The level of satisfaction is expected to increase the level of institutional commitment (pp. 158-160).

Although Bean was able to account for only 21 percent of the variance in dropout for females and 12 percent for males at the one university where he attempted to test his model, the relationships were generally in the expected direction. For example, commitment to the institution made the largest contribution to explaining retention and attrition for both men and women. Furthermore, a variable was found to be significantly related to retention and attrition that had never been examined before in the collegiate setting—routinization. Routinization is the degree to which the role of being a worker or student is viewed as repetitive (which might imply boredom).

In summary, theory and research both demonstrate the importance of student-institution interaction variables as factors that relate to and explain retention and attrition. And as demonstrated by Bean's hypothesis regarding routinization, a focus on the interaction and fit between students and their institution may stimulate thinking about additional, potentially useful variables that have not been examined before.

Action Strategies to Improve Retention

In this chapter an attempt will be made to integrate the findings of two types of studies in order to draw the best possible conclusions about how to improve student retention on a college or university campus: (1) studies exploring the relationships between retention/ attrition and student, institutional, and interaction factors (see chapter 2 and Lenning, Beal, and Sauer 1980); and (2) empirical exploration of action strategies and their observed impacts on retention (see Beal and Noel 1980). However, a word of caution should be mentioned: obtaining the highest possible retention rate is not necessarily the most desirable goal. Some students need to transfer, stop out, or drop out for their own benefit, and an approach that could somehow force them to stay would be inappropriate, in spite of the detrimental financial implications of decreased enrollment. Haagen (1977) cites numerous cases where it was beneficial for a student to leave. Even "upward bound" programs have recognized this: "the student who leaves school in order to think things through or to weigh whether or not he really wants a college education is making an attempt at mature decision making" (Princeton Cooperative School Program 1977, p. 9). Rather than improving retention per se, the primary goal should be to better meet student needs and to provide a more meaningful educational experience. And in the long run, motivations closer to the mission of the institution probably will lead to higher enrollments and tuition revenue than will a short-sighted, survivalist focus on enrollments for enrollments' sake.

The following section describes the design of the "What Works in Student Retention?" (WWISR) study conducted jointly by the National Center for Higher Education Management Systems (NCHEMS) and the American College Testing program (ACT). The final two sections of this chapter integrate the findings of the WWISR study with the other research found in the literature and extrapolate generalizations about how to improve student retention.

The WWISR study

After appropriate developmental and field-test activities, a postcard questionnaire was sent in early 1979 to the presidents of all 2,459 accredited undergraduate colleges and universities in the United States. The questionnaire asked several basic questions about retention at their institutions, including whether they would like to participate in an in-depth survey of how institutions were trying to improve retention.

A total of 1,600 presidents responded favorably, and eventually 947 usable, completed, in-depth questionnaires were received. Respondents indicated retention rates for their campuses, types of retention analyses they had done, factors they believed to be most important in student retention, and special action programs that were being implemented to improve retention. Those having action programs were asked to complete a separate activity report form for *each program*. They were asked to describe the program in detail and to indicate evidence of its success or lack of success in influencing student retention. A total of 1,024 such report forms were received from 387 institutions.

An index of retention success was developed, and each action program was given a retention success rating based on content analysis by three judges. The scale of the index ranged from one (no increase in retention) to five (great improvement.)* For all 913 programs for which a retention success index was calculated, the mean index was 1.96. For the 420 programs that experienced at least some positive retention impact (those receiving a rating of two or more), the mean index was 3.33. A total of 49 programs received a rating of five, and Beal and Noel (1980) provide a brief description of each of these "exemplary programs." For more information on the design of the study and for findings in addition to those reported in the next two sections of this chapter, see Beal and Noel (1980).

Single-facet retention approaches

Approaches concerned with improving retention can be narrow in scope or broad and multifaceted. This section discusses the perceived utility of various single-facet approaches. The approaches for which at least some success is indicated have been grouped into a dozen categories plus an "other" category.

Admissions and recruiting. The relationship of admissions and recruiting to retention has been largely neglected until recently. Seemingly, the primary concern of most recruiters and admissions people, as discussed in the earlier literature, was to get prospective students enrolled, "in the door," with little thought to recruiting for retention. This practice is a major reason for the

---

*All institutions reporting a retention improvement of ten or more percentage points after implementation of the program were given a rating of five. Institutions that did not report a percentage change but reported they had observed "great improvement" were also given a rating of five.

Theodore Lownik Library
Illinois Benedictine College
Lisle Illinois 60532

preponderance of what some have termed "revolving college doors." Although the federal government has devoted most of its attention to improving access to education, in the middle '70s significant federal funds were devoted to facilitating the improvement of student choice of institution. Some of these funds made possible a series of cooperative projects to help institutions know what institutional and program information students need to make informed decisions that would be satisfying to them and best allow their educational needs to be met (El-Khawas 1978). The projects also focused on how institutions can communicate effectively such information to different groups of prospective students. As stated by Lenning and Cooper (1978):

> Information that postsecondary institutions provide to prospective students is often incomplete, insufficiently detailed, not clearly presented, or presented at the wrong time. [The authors later provided documentation of this charge.] The failure to provide adequate information can result in an unwise choice of institutions or programs of study and, consequently, low student morale, high attrition rates, and future recruiting problems for the institution (p. vii).

Student retention and recruitment are actually "two sides of the same coin." If students receive adequate information from colleges, they will be more likely to choose institutions that meet their needs, which in turn will increase their chances of persisting. If students regret their choice of college, and especially if they feel that the information provided by the institution misled them, they will tend to resent the college and tell their peers of their experiences, which could negatively affect future recruiting.

The federal government also has devoted large sums of money to developing computerized information systems (Green 1977) and to helping prospective students ask the right questions of institutions (Hamilton, Wolff, and Dayton 1976). Messages for prospective students developed by the latter project were broadcast during 1980 as public service announcements by radio and television stations around the country.

The importance of keeping student retention in mind during the recruitment and admissions processes has been recognized by a number of special retention program developers (Simmons and Maxwell-Simmons 1978; Martinez 1978; Hayden et al. 1976; McDermott 1975; Marchbanks 1974; Heath et al. 1973). Several of these programs are being aimed specifically at minority populations. For guidelines and helpful examples in this area see Chapman, Griffith, and Johnson (1979), El-Khawas (1978), Leach (1978), Lenning and Cooper (1978), and Stark (1978).

Advising. The research on interactions between students and faculty and students and their peers suggests that advising conducted by faculty and/or peers would be desirable if the relationship is one of quality (which suggests the need for careful selection and training of advisors). Furthermore, effective advising would be expected to contribute to the students' self-confidence and sense of where they are going in their college careers, a student characteristic that has been found to be related positively to retention. The WWISR study results confirm this. "Inadequate academic advising" was reported by campuses to be the most important reason for attrition, and "high quality of advising" was ranked fifth in importance as a contributor to student retention. Furthermore, advising as an action program for improving retention has been implemented by 61 institutions and, more often than not, had been found to contribute to retention.

Where such programs were most successful in improving retention, the advisory staff consisted of carefully selected and trained faculty or professional advisors. In some cases, advising by student peers also was used. Evaluating and providing rewards for good advising was found to be important in one program. In many cases the program focused primarily on freshman and transfers; in others it was an on-going process. In some cases an advising center was set up, but more often the program was not centralized in that manner. In some cases the program was combined with other programs, such as orientation, and diagnostic assessment was used. However, the special advising programs that influenced retention usually were long term and on-going.

Turning to the research literature, Kesselman (1976) found in a survey of deans that although 95 percent of undergraduate students consider dropping out at one time or another, only one out of three seeks advice from professors. This suggests that getting students to use the advisory program can be a problem, which may be the reason peer advisors become important for advisory assistance and referral to professional advisors. Clearly, selection and training are important also, as is providing adequate time for advisors to conduct such activities. Rossmann (1968) found at one private college that merely giving released time to faculty for advising did not improve retention, but students seemed more satisfied with their advisors. Perhaps he also would have found an effect on retention if effective selection and training of advisors had been part of the program. For example, in a special retention program at Drake University (1974), exit-prone freshmen who received significant advising time from ranked faculty members participating in the "humanistic advising-training program" had a higher retention rate than the freshmen class as a whole. Faculty not interested in advising should not be forced into it but the support of the president and top administration for such activities is an important motivator, especially if coupled with other incentives such as released time.

Counseling. Counseling is intended to affect positively self-concept, motivation, values clarification, perceptions of and relationships to others, involvement, and the academic and personal adjustment and problems (with associated anxiety and stress) that have been found by various research studies to affect student attrition and retention. In large part, the effect of counseling on student retention is determined by the extent to which counseling activities, in a particular setting and with specific personnel working with students having specific needs, are able to influence such factors.

Counseling has served as a foundation for numerous retention programs—for example, see Simmons and Maxwell-Simmons (1978), Appel et al. (1977), Dallas (1971), Montes and Ortega (1976), McDermott (1975), West et al. (1975), Lee (1974), Heath et al. (1973), Reimanis (1973), and Fishman and Dugan (n.d.).

For an example of the positive impact of personal counseling in 11 of the NORCAL colleges (Macmillan and Kester 1973) experimental design studies tested the implementation of intervention strategies. At all 11 colleges, student retention was significantly improved, and they all had employed special counseling (either individual or group) directed at potential dropouts. This success prompted the NORCAL coordinators, Macmillan and Kester, to assert that attrition can be halved. However, the survey by Kesselman (1976) suggests that only one in ten students considering withdrawal ever contacts a counselor for help in thinking through what to do. Thus, the effectiveness of the program in dealing with students does not necessarily mean as much success as it might seem on the surface. Students must be motivated to participate in the program.

Noel (1976) has pointed out that the first six months of enrollment are especially critical, and counseling service intervention can play a vital role. Papke (1978) documents that pre-enrollment counseling can be effective in improving retention. White's (1971) research at Montgomery College (a two-year college) suggests the desirability of designing differential counseling approaches to deal with the varying psychological syndrome of dropout-prone students. Reimanis (1973) reports on a program at Corning Community College that successfully reduced attrition through weekly "rap" sessions for Educational Opportunity Program students, a short course in achievement motivation training, locus-of-control counseling, group counseling for high-anxiety nursing students, and encounter groups to improve the self-concept of students. The underlying theme in all these programs was that the faculty and administration showed their genuine interest in the students' personal and academic growth. Furthermore, the programs were successful because they involved good coordination and communication and were targeted toward specific groups and problems. On the other hand, Vest and Spino (1975) contended many colleges could improve their retention percentage as much as 10 percent if they did not offer such a confusing and overabundant array of counseling programs, but instead consolidated programs with better coordination, cooperation, and communication.

Following up on the targeting idea, Schotzinger, Buchanan, and Fahrenback (1976) found a peer counseling program for commuter students to be effective, Montes and Ortego (1976) found that peer counseling for nontraditional students worked, and Grites (1979) reviewed several targeted counseling programs (sometimes it is difficult to differentiate counseling from advising) that improved student retention. Successful programs can be individual or group counseling as referred to above, seminars (Silver 1978), or courses such as Adams' (1974) career planning course. They can take place in the counseling center, a dormitory, or some other accessible location.

Dallas's successful program (1971) at Napa College also deserves special mention because of the initiative, accessibility, flexibility, and caring that was built in. As summarized by Beal and Noel (1980):

> The purpose of this project was to establish a "someone cares" atmosphere. The counselor took the initiative to request students to drop in for counseling and initiated outreach for those who did not drop in. The program emphasized immediate accessibility and included informal contact anywhere on the campus. The counselors directed interviews that explored life goals, abilities, and interests, course and program requirements, time scheduling, course scheduling, and use of campus resources. Comparison with students in a control group showed that those with special counseling services had a lower attrition rate, a higher enrollment rate, a higher grade point average, and completed more units (p. 11).

The WWISR study generally confirms the importance of counseling, where needed, to increase retention. Counseling tied for ninth among action programs (with peer programs and dropout studies) in terms of the impact on retention as indicated by the "retention index" used in the study. As emphasized by O'Brien (1967), colleges need improved ways to induce students to seek counseling. One way may be to get away from the stigma that many lay people associate with the term counseling; perhaps we need a different name for this activity. Another potential strategy is to bring counseling opportunities to where students live and work.

Early warning and prediction. Leon (1975), in a small study of Chicano students, discovered that they went through four phases in developing a dropout rationale, and that intervention by the college, to be effective, should occur in as early a phase as possible, and certainly prior to Phase 4—the adoption of a rationale for withdrawing. Students need help as they decide whether to leave and as they start developing a dropout rationale. However, another study of the withdrawal process involving more typical students (Chickering and Hannah 1969) discovered there was minimal interaction with institutional personnel during the entire withdrawal process. Instead, peers and parents were reported to be the withdrawing students' confidants.

In response to this finding, three strategies could be employed: direct the retention program at *all* students; direct the program at specific groups of students (for example, minority students); and identify potential dropouts and target efforts toward them, including motivating them to take part in these efforts. Regarding the third strategy, Heath et al. (1973) contend that procedures should be established *at admissions time* to assist potential dropouts. Other equally important times are when students decide upon or change majors, experience academic difficulty, drop courses, or request transcripts. We would say that potential dropouts should be identified as early as possible, even prior to admissions, if feasible, so that special summer skill-building and motivational sessions can be used.

Numerous institutions have tried to identify potential dropouts and help them overcome obstacles that could prevent them from persisting, but such predictions often have not proven to be very accurate for other than those dropping out because of low grades. For predicting academic dropouts due to low grades, college grades earned during the first semester are the best predictors. Pedrini and Pedrini (n.d., 1976) found that college grades were the only significant predicator for black students at the University of Nebraska at Omaha regardless of income level, while ACT scores and financial aid receipt also were significant predictors for other students. They concluded that any predictor variables other than college grades were unreliable.

On the other hand, if pre-admissions prediction is desired— so that college orientation sessions and pre-college counseling can be targeted, for example—high school rank or grade point average and college admissions test scores become useful predictors. Lee (1974), in a study of a special retention program for academically disadvantaged students at Middlesex Community College, found six characteristics of disadvantaged students that often lead to failure and that must be addressed by the action program: (1) they tend to be poorly motivated or to have unrealistic motivations and goals; (2) they usually are unrealistic about the time they will need to complete their program, not recognizing that it will take three years to complete a two-year program; (3) they often have emotional problems that undermine their self-confidence and result in a "what's the use" attitude; (4) they are poor readers; (5) they tend to have problems thinking in abstract terms and using deductive reasoning and depend more on real life experience than symbolic experience in developing their ideas; and (6) they and their parents are often suspicious of intellectuals.

At most colleges the percentage of those withdrawing voluntarily is larger than those who are forced to withdraw because of low grades, although the percentage varies for different colleges and types of students (Tinto and Cullen 1973; Jaffe and Adams 1970). For example, Panos and Astin (1968) found in their national sample of students that about three-fourths of those withdrawing dropped out voluntarily. Similarly, Astin (1975c) reports that only 22 percent of his national sample of dropouts gave poor grades as a reason for dropping out (28 percent for men and 14 percent for women). Chickering and Hannah (1969) reported that most of the dropouts in their sample of small colleges were voluntary, and Johansson and Rossmann (1973) found 80 percent of the female dropouts and half of the male dropouts at Macalester College to be voluntary. Brigman and Stager (1980) reported that the National Longitudinal Study of the High School Class of 1972 found that "freshman-year voluntary withdrawals exceeded academic dismissals by ratios of 2 to 1 in four-year colleges and 4 to 1 in two-year colleges." (p. 1). They also concluded that the ratio has been increasing during the past 15 years, which suggests that the 45 percent voluntary freshman dropouts figure found in 1966 for the University of California, Berkeley (Rossmann and Kirk 1970) is probably far below the percentage that would be found at Berkeley today.

A probable reason why so many attempts to predict voluntary dropouts have been unsuccessful is that student demographic variables were used as the predictors. For example, Vogt (1977) found poor prediction using 19 demographic variables and hypothesized that subjective information about student attitudes and educational goals was needed. Lanning (1977) suggested that the common failure to predict potential dropouts with "traditional variables" means that we need to uncover "personal reasons" for dropping out. Another possible reason suggested by Michlein (1977), in a study of technical institutes throughout

Wisconsin, was his finding that the factors related to retention and attrition varied from institution to institution and within the institution from program to program. He concluded that differential diagnosis of student characteristics is needed for accurate prediction, and that such identification of potential dropouts necessitates an undue amount of work that is not cost effective. In their national study, which included some motivational variables, Peng and Fetters (1977) also did not obtain good predictions, which they concluded was because attrition is a complex process that functions differently in different people. Of course, theirs was also a study across many types of institutions and programs, which could have been the reason their predictions were not good.

All is not bleak with regard to predicting retention, however, either in terms of effectiveness or of cost in staff time and effort. In the successful NORCAL project for reducing attrition at 23 community colleges in northern California (Macmillan and Kester 1973), a model predictive instrument was developed that was found useful over a three-year period at most of the colleges, with a "hit rate" of 68 percent being experienced at one of the colleges (for both voluntary and involuntary dropouts as a combined group). The accuracy of prediction guided college officials in designing the action programs as well as in helping them to identify those students to whom the program should be targeted. Predictive variables included race, family affluence, concern about matters of finance and employment, amount of parental encouragement for their pursuit of college, personal importance attached to college, educational aspirations, and ability.

Blanchfield (1971) found multiple discriminant analysis to predict attrition with good results (70 to 73 percent predictive accuracy) at Syracuse University when both pre-college and college environmental variables were used. Social Consciousness Test (an instrument published by the Educational Testing Service) scores, percentage of college costs financed by grants, and high school rank were the best predictors of retention and attrition. Neely (1977) also found some success with discriminant analysis. Two other very recent studies (Pascarella and Terenzini 1980; and Terenzini, Lorang, and Pascarella 1980) obtained phenomenal results using multiple discriminant analysis, but it was much more than the statistical method that made the difference. Furthermore, when predicting membership in dichotomous categories (such as persister versus withdrawer), multiple regression analysis should give the same results (Kerlinger and Pedazur 1973). If more than two categories of persistence-withdrawal are being used (for example, academic withdrawers, voluntary withdrawers, and persisters), clearly multiple discriminant analysis should be the choice.

In the two most recent prediction studies referred to above, the first was conducted for students at Syracuse University (private) and the other was a replication using students at the State University of New York at Albany. A 34-item multidimensional questionnaire was developed that was intended to assess the major dimensions of Tinto's (1975) model of student retention:

> The constructs of students' integration into the social and academic systems of an institution are at the model's conceptual core. Tinto conceived of the college student attrition process as a series of socio-psychological interactions between the characteristics students bring with them to college and the nature of their experiences while enrolled. According to Tinto, students' pre-college traits lead to varying initial levels of goal and institutional commitments which, in turn, interact with the academic and social environment of the institution, resulting in varying levels of integration in the institution's social and academic systems.... Academic integration may manifest itself in the student's academic performance, sense of intellectual development, sharing the intellectual or academic values of peers and faculty members, and so on. Similarly, indicators of social integration include frequency and quality of contacts with peers, a sense of shared values in nonacademic areas, and involvement in the non-classroom life of the institution. While the model places interactions with faculty in the domain of social integration, Tinto states that such interactions are also likely to enhance academic integration ... levels of social and academic integration are influenced by pre-college characteristics and level of commitment [that]... in turn, mediate subsequent levels of commitment to completing college [that in turn affects]... the likelihood of continued enrollment in the institution (Terezini, Lorang, and Pascarella 1980, pp. 1 and 5).

For each item in the instrument, students responded to a scale of 5 (strongly agree) to 1 (strongly disagree), and applying factor analysis to student responses yielded five instrument dimension scales with generally acceptable statistical reliability. (Mean alpha reliability coefficients across the two studies for the five scales were .84, .83, .77, .72, and .65, respectively.) The factor structure was almost the same for the two universities, suggesting its appropriateness for institutions with different characteristics and types of students.

The five scales, along with an indication of the number of items belonging to each scale and one or two items that weighed the most on each scale, are listed below:

I. Peer Group Relations (7 items)
   Since coming to this university I have developed close personal relationships with other students.

The student friendships I have developed at this university have been personally satisfying.

II. Informal Interactions with Faculty (5 items)
My non-classroom interactions with faculty have had a positive influence on my personal growth, values, and attitudes.
My non-classroom interactions with faculty have had a positive influence on my career goals and aspirations.

III. Faculty Concern for Student Development and Teaching (5 items)
Few of the faculty members I have had contact with are genuinely interested in students.

IV. Academic and Intellectual Development (7 items)
I am satisfied with the extent of my intellectual development since enrolling in this institution.

V. Institutional/Goal Commitments (6 items)
It is important for me to graduate from college.

In both studies, any potential effects of the following pre-college characteristics were cancelled out (controlled for) before trying to predict (based on the five scale scores) whether each entering student would persist through the freshman year:

- sex
- minority member or not
- enrolled initially in liberal arts or professional program ·
- Scholastic Aptitude Test total score
- high school rank
- parents' combined annual income
- mother's formal education
- father's formal education
- highest academic degree expected
- whether the university was the student's first, second, third, fourth, lower choice
- freshman year cumulative grade point average
- extent of involvement as freshman in extracurricular activities

Controlled for in the first study but not the second were:

- high school extracurricular involvement
- expected frequency of contact with faculty members
- pre-matriculation importance of graduating from college
- pre-registration confidence that the decision to attend this university was the right one

In the first study of Syracuse University freshmen, after the prediction equations had been developed using the majority of the freshmen, they were applied to predicting withdrawal status of an independent cross-validation sample of freshmen who had been randomly selected and taken out of the total group ahead of time. From this sample 79 percent of the persisters and 76 percent of the voluntary leavers were correctly classified by the prediction equations. At SUNY-Albany, 75 percent of the persisters in the cross-validation sample were correctly identified. Since there were no voluntary dropouts in the cross-validation sample, the predictive accuracy for this category could not be determined. (The predictive accuracy was 64 percent correct using the calibration sample on which the equations were developed.)

The final two studies above give real hope that college personnel will be able to easily and efficiently identify potential voluntary dropouts and persisters very early. This is especially true if such identification is used in conjunction with an on-going, flexible, computer-based, cohort-survival information system, like the one at California State University, Northridge that is described by Newlon and Gaither (1980).

Two other studies add to the promise of being able to easily and usefully predict student persistence and voluntary attrition. Johnson and Chapman (1980) had 2,410 freshmen at 11 diverse two- and four-year institutions respond to a special questionnaire on demographic/personality characteristics, educational commitment, and involvement in academic and social activities. Multiple discriminant analysis was used to ascertain factors differentiating those returning the second semester from those not returning. The findings for men and women were different, as were the findings for four-year colleges and community colleges, but they seemed to support Tinto's model. What is important for this discussion, however, is that, across the board, the best predictor of "leavers" was to ask students if they intended to return to campus the next semester. Forty percent who said they would not return the second semester did not return. A substantial number of potential dropouts evidently can be identified through the simple process of asking students about their plans to leave or remain.

The final study to be discussed concerns dropping out of, or persisting in, an academic course. Using data from four open-learning courses on campuses of the Chicago City Colleges, Giltrow and Duby (1976) developed a formula that was able to predict course-completion status with an accuracy of plus or minus 10 percent for seven out of eight cases. The best predictors were student sex, the campus at which the student registered, and whether the student returned assigned questionnaires. Although we have some question about this study, it does suggest that potentially useful withdraw/persist predictions are also possible at the course level. (Our questioning of the study is based on whether such accuracy is possible with dichotomous predictor variables.)

Our discussion throughout this section has been on early warning resulting from prediction rather than on the action follow-up. The follow-up probably will need to be one or a combination of the action efforts discussed in the other sections. A discussion of early warning is appropriate here, however, because it is a part of the action strategy. Furthermore, in the WWISR study early warning systems ranked fourth in terms of reported action program impact on retention.

Exit interviews. Exit interviews generally are conducted to gather information about why students leave and what changes the institution needs to make to improve retention for other students. Demos (1968) found, however, that 10 percent of the students planning to drop out decided against doing so after being involved in exit interviews with trained counselors. This suggests that interviews can serve an action role in reducing attrition, and the WWISR study found that 15 responding institutions reported exit interviews as specific action programs. Even though their observed impact on retention ranked the lowest of 15 action programs listed, some positive impact was found on retention rates. Furthermore, in many cases the impact of exit interviews might have been improved if the interview had not been left until the last minute, when it might be perceived by the student as an imposition or inconvenience.

Extracurricular activities. By extracurricular activieis we are referring to activities that are outside the formal college curriculum, but that may supplement the formal curriculum and allow students to try out and test things they have learned. Additional learning that may be as beneficial as that learned in the formal academic program also can take place through extracurricular activities, which is why some have termed this sphere the "cocurriculum." Since extracurricular activities actively involve students in the life of the institution, it would be expected that more often than not meaningful participation in extracurricular activities would contribute to student retention. A number of studies have found just that (Bean 1980; Everett 1979; Michlein 1977; Tinto 1975; McDermott 1975; Kamens 1972; Chase 1970; Schmid and Reed 1966; Sexton 1965). For example, in her study of Pennsylvania State University students, Everett (1979) found that 79 percent of the persisters had participated in at least one extracurricular activity, compared to only 42 percent of the dropouts. Furthermore, the differences were even more marked for particular activity areas: intramurals and sports clubs, 54 percent to 25 percent; special-interest organizations, 38 percent to 14 percent; professional and honorary societies, 15 percent to 1 percent.

Faculty play an important role in determining the effectiveness of the contribution of extracurricular activities to retention, as was implied in the preceding chapter. As indicated there, both the frequency and quality of faculty-student interactions outside the classroom are crucial to student retention, especially the interaction quality (Terenzini and Pascarella 1980; Terenzini, Lorang, and Pascarella 1980). Non-faculty personnel not directly involved in coordinating extracurricular activities (including administrators, secretaries, and custodians) can also play an important role in improving retention if they can be made aware of their potential impact and be provided with in-service training and motivation for serving in such a role. Motivation is often provided through incentives such as recognizing the person's contribution and expressing appreciation for it at appropriate opportunities. As found by Panos and Astin (1968), a total campus atmosphere of warmth, friendliness, and sincere caring means greater student retention, all other factors being equal. And as pointed out by William Moore (1976), a negative attitude toward disadvantaged, remedial students—a lack of appreciation for them as persons—by other individuals on campus outside the developmental program can have a catastrophic effect on the academic success of such students.

In the WWISR study, "inadequate extracurricular offerings" was one of the top negative campus characteristics considered to be related to retention, and "student involvement in campus life" one of the top positive characteristics. On the other hand, relatively few institutions emphasized the development of extracurricular activities for improving student retention. Also, the programs that were attempted were rated rather low in their impact on retention. Based on the research literature reviewed in the preceding chapter, colleges should be concerned with the quality and effectiveness of programs offered. They should: stimulate campus organizations to be more active in seeking out students and to understand their part in serving as a motivational force for retention (Michlein 1977); offer activities that are varied enough to meet diverse interests and the particular social, personal, and career development needs and goals of different individuals in a manner that is comfortable and inviting to them; effect linkages between the curricular and extracurricular; organize activities in a manner so that close friendships can develop; offer activities so that they lead to an increased feeling by the participating student of being an important part of the college and its campus life; provide opportunities, both formal and informal, for students with like interests, needs, or characteristics to have interactions that are meaningful to them (e.g., a black students club); arrange faculty and staff availability by creating opportunities for interaction with students.

While it is important for students to be active and involved, it is the quality and nature of involvement rather than the frequency that is crucial, as reported in Heath et al. (1973). It is also possible that students can be so involved in extracurricular activities that their persistence is adversely affected. For example, Demitroff (1974) found that students who withdrew had spent more time participating in extracurricular activities, and also thought them more important, than did the students who persisted.

Faculty, staff, and curricular development. The major reason most students are in college is to obtain a quality education that meets important personal and career needs. For this to happen to the greatest extent possible, appropriate selection and in-service development of faculty, staff, and curriculum must occur. As indicated by Flannery et al. (1973, p. 6), "it is the instructors who ultimately make the educational system effective and relevant and they must accept the responsibility of using the resources of the college to help students." After completing his review of the literature, Rowell (1974) concluded that a personalized approach to education and personal problems is a key to good student retention because it helps make students more comfortable and pleased with their educational environment. Heath et al., (1973, pp. 6-7) stated effectively and in specific terms a number of the things that faculty can do to affect student retention in a positive manner:

> The faculty can encourage persistence by the quality of their teaching (creative, innovative methods), by their quality as persons (understanding selves as well as understanding students), by their attitudes (toward the students, the college, and other faculty), by ending subtle discouragement, and by establishing and expecting *reasonable* standards and fulfilling their responsibility to those standards. . . . They *must* become more involved with total student development. Contradictions in students' value systems should be examined and resolved perhaps by using human development seminars. . . . Presidential support is needed, but the key to faculty involvement is the Dean of the Faculty. . . . Faculty applicants need to be carefully screened and current ones should have inservice training (maybe points toward promotion and pay increases given for participation). If peer counselors are used for recruiting, faculty should be incorporated into their training sessions. . . . Personal attention from someone on the staff, individualized learning approaches and staff development have been successful techniques. Have *logical* rules and regula-

tions. Be sure *all* facets of the college present some warmth and interest toward students. Sense new needs of students as they arise. The college should aim for a *total* climate conducive to learning and development.... The faculty can identify potential failures for counselors to help.... The faculty should serve as contacts with high schools, serve as summer advisors, participate with counselors to create learning resources, teach to the needs of students, and use non-punitive grading.

To carry out these tasks effectively, many faculty need training assistance. Thus, for example, Heath et al. (1973) concluded that faculty need to be *taught* how to make better referrals to counselors.

The crucial role that faculty can play outside the classroom discussed earlier, should be mentioned again here. Student out-of-class interaction with faculty to whom they can readily relate as "real persons" contributes to the probability that faculty can be role models (Walton 1979, emphasizes the special importance of such models for ethnic minority students) and "significant others" (Husband 1976; Noel 1976; Schulman 1976). Through faculty efforts, the extracurriculum can supplement and test out concepts and principles taught by the faculty in class. In-service orientation and training for faculty on how to improve such roles and how to work more effectively with student affairs staff are important because these topics are outside the realm of the faculty members' graduate school training.

Faculty development seminars and other activities using appropriate incentives for participation and involvement (including involvement in planning the activities) were found useful in several retention programs reported in the literature (Simmons and Maxwell-Simmons 1978; Branch 1975; McDermott 1975; West et al. 1975; and Reimanis 1973). Reimanis (1973) focused on how to make classrooms student-centered in his in-service faculty program, and he also provided technical faculty with information about affective/confluent education principles. For a "more than cost effective" community college program for academically disadvantaged minority students, West et al. (1975) particularly emphasized the importance of using open-ended, humanistic instructional techniques, coupled with performance objectives and criterion-referenced standards that are structured. Teaching style and methodology are important, and the needs vary with the types of students, their learning styles (Cross 1976), whether they are conforming or independence-oriented students (Domino 1970), and other factors (Schalock 1976). The success, in terms of student retention, of tailoring instructional style and methodology to particular groups of students has been demonstrated by various programs (Reiser and Sullivan 1978; Anandam, 1977; Appel et al.

1977; Rouche and Mink 1975; West et al., 1975). For example, the experience of West et al. (1975) suggested to them that for all their developmental courses targeted at minority students, the following special methods are important to retention: (1) warm personal relationships, (2) small classes of 15 to 25, (3) use of audiovisual equipment, (4) individualized instruction that allows students to proceed at their own pace, (5) video-taping classes and playing them back, (6) an open-ended behavioral emphasis, (7) nonpunitive grading, and (8) a humanistic classroom atmosphere.

Curricular variety, design, and choice are also important to student retention (E. Moore 1976; Astin 1975c; McGuckin and Winkler 1974; Fishman and Dugan n.d.). As with teaching methodology, it is important to tailor curriculum to the specific needs of the different types of students.

The WWISR study supports the generalizations extracted from the research literature concerning faculty, staff, and curricular development. "Caring attitude of faculty and staff," "high quality of teaching," and "high quality of advising" were campus factors most often reported in WWISR to be related to student *retention.* "Inadequate curricular offerings," "inadequate academic advising," and "conflict between class schedule and job" were the campus factors reported most often related to *attrition.* "Curricular developments" and "faculty/staff development" were action programs that ranked high in their ability to influence student retention positively. Furthermore, a number of the special programs referred to as exemplary because of their observed impact on retention had faculty and staff development as a major component.

Financial aid. Financial problems commonly are given by those withdrawing as a primary reason for leaving the institution, and such problems may or may not be an underlying reason. Both Demos (1968) and Demitroff (1974) concluded that some students give this reason mainly because it is socially acceptable. In a study of the Minnesota State Colleges, Fenstemacher (1973) found that such reasons were related to a reluctance to apply for financial aid. Nevertheless, it was found in well-designed studies by Astin (1975b, 1975c) and Blanchfield (1971) that scholarships and grants relate positively to student retention irrespective of ability, and loans (especially large ones) relate negatively to retention. Findings reported by Wenc (1977), Heath et al. (1973), Pedrini and Pedrini (n.d.), and Nelson (1966) support such a conclusion. However, a national study by Peng and Fetters (1977) and studies by Fields and LeMay (1973), Selby (1973), and Eckland (1964) did not find such a relationship. Thus, it would appear that financial aid can have positive effects on student retention, depending on how the students view the aid (for example, does it give security and give a positive self-image in relation to the college).

Astin (1975b, 1975c) also studied employment, and it would appear from his study and others that part-time employment or work-study (under 25 hours) can positively affect retention, especially if the work is on-campus, the student starts work as a freshman, and the student is not married (part-time work related negatively to retention for married students). Since satisfaction with the work was not found to be related to persistence, Astin concluded that a key to its impact was that it provided an involvement with campus life and interaction with others on campus. Working off-campus, working full time, and/or working in the field of study were related to attrition according to Astin's findings.

Assistance in obtaining financial support was an important component in two successful retention programs found in the literature (West et al. 1975; Lee 1974). Furthermore, in the WWISR study, "inadequate financial aid" was reported to be the fourth most important negative factor and "adequate financial aid" the third most important positive factor in influencing retention. On the other hand, only one of the several dozen action programs rated as exemplary because of the observed effect on student retention had financial aid and part-time employment as a major component.

Housing. Many studies have demonstrated that living in dormitories, and often even more in fraternities and sororities, improved a student's chances of retention (Astin 1975c; Kuznik 1975; Chickering 1974; DiCesare, Sedlacek and Brooks 1972; Nasatir 1969; Bolyard and Martin 1973; and Alfert 1966). Special living-learning arrangements can improve retention (Terenzini and Pascarella 1980b), as can matching roommates or groupings within living units based on student background and other characteristics (Kuznik 1975; Nasatir 1969; Brown 1968). Based on the literature review of the previous chapter, retention in a living unit can be enhanced through involving more students in meaningful residential activities and arranging the setting to stimulate or promote quality student-student and student-faculty discussion and other interactions. Chickering (1974) discusses a variety of ways in which campus housing can be improved to more effectively promote active student life, educational involvement, and retention. Although living units were not a focus in any of the retention action programs identified by WWISR, the literature clearly supports the positive potential of residential programs.

Learning and academic support. During the past decade, there has been an influx of learning centers on campuses across the country. Originally they were designed specifically to aid in remedial or developmental work; to help students (especially entering students) who were deficient in the basic learning skills (such as study skills, reading, writing, etc.) or who had fears and anxieties keeping them from functioning as effective students. The learning centers used skills laboratories with sophisticated audiovisual equipment to assist developmental students. Basic skills courses were offered, some for credit but often for no credit, and tutoring and counseling often were provided.

Today, many learning centers have expanded into learning assistance roles targeted at all students. In addition, they sometimes assist in curriculum development, provide faculty with audiovisual equipment and materials for teaching and improving teaching methods, and conduct in-service training for the effective use of the equipment and materials. Clearly, learning centers can have a major role in student retention as well as in improving academic competencies and instruction (Lenning and Mayman, forthcoming).

The type of assistance offered by academic support programs, such as learning centers, varies widely, for example: academic support program specifically for minorities (Simmons and Maxwell-Simmons 1978); a block scheduled cooperative learning program of special courses, tutoring, and counseling (Fishman and Dugan n.d.); an individualized interpersonal and interdisciplinary team approach (Aarons 1975); five special courses taught using a team approach (Bochniarz 1978) an interdisciplinary remedial core program focusing on language skills (Buckley 1976); peer modeling and counseling (Montes and Ortega 1976); a self-development seminar (Silver 1978); and special summer pre-enrollment sessions of skill-building and motivational aids (Lee 1974). In the case of the program reported by Bochniarz (1978), student retention for the special program was better than that of the regular remedial program only for the first semester, although those in the special program attained higher grades over the entire three years of the study. In this interdisciplinary team program, the retention rates of those students who volunteered to participate in the program were the same as for those students pressured into participation. This suggests that it is warranted to pressure probable dropouts to participate, using appropriate positive and negative incentives.

After reviewing national studies indicating that remedial and developmental programs in community colleges had, in general, been unsuccessful, Rouche and Mink (1975) hypothesized that this lack of success was because these programs were not built around individualized, learner-oriented instructional concepts where there is a systematic design of the total learning environment, multiple entry levels into carefully ordered curricular sequences, personal and professional involvement by staff, and an open approach to specific problems on a generalized, fundamental level. Preliminary results of their project have indicated that at least one semester of such individualized instruction does shift students effectively toward an internal locus of control. Also supporting such conclusions is the finding in an experimental study by Carman (n.d.) that a remedial program involving programed materials had a significant impact on student retention only because tutoring was a part of the program. Perhaps directors of state-supported developmental programs at colleges throughout Ohio took such advice to heart, because a study of these programs (Ohio State-Wide Advisory Committee on Developmental Education 1976) concluded that generally such programs had yielded "substantial, measurable improvement" in basic skills, college grades, retention rates, and accomplishment of personal growth objectives.

Whether it is a part of a learning center program or not, tutoring—and especially tutoring of minority and other disadvantaged students lacking basic skills—has been found to assist retention at a number of institutions (National Academy of Sciences-National Research Council 1977; West et al. 1975; Lee 1974; MacMillan and Kester 1973; Heath et al. 1973; Carman n.d.; Fishman and Dugan n.d.). Older, more experienced students can be effective as tutors because they are peers to whom the students can relate, particularly if they are of the same race. Training in how to tutor effectively is imperative.

Emphasizing the importance of academic learning support programs is the WWISR study finding that such action programs were ranked second in terms of their impact on student retention. Clearly their increasingly widespread acceptance and implementation across the country are warranted, assuming that Rouche and Mink's (1975) concerns and recommendations are heeded.

Orientation. New, entering students undoubtedly feel the need for, and can benefit greatly from, activities orienting them to their new educational environment, to others' expectations of them, to the institution's rules and regulations, etc. Yet, in the past, too many orientation programs relied on poorly designed, "one-shot" beginning-of-the-year talks and activities that were the same for everyone. Older students, minorities, and transfer students received exactly the same orientation. Often little attempt was made to meet differential needs in such programs. This is probably why orientation programs often have had no impact on retention. Some institutions that have redesigned their orientation programs have had marked improvements in their retention rates.

Many of the correlational findings reported in chapter two imply strategies for orientation programs. For example, the program should allow students and peers to interact and get to know one another and should provide informal interactions between faculty and students. In orientation programs warmth and friendliness should predominate, educational and occupational goals and aspirations should be explored and assistance given to help clarify them, individual and group needs and expectations should be discussed and responded to as appropriate, financial aid and employment opportunities and potential benefits should be discussed, and a sense of caring should prevail. The programs should involve a systematic, developmental series of activities over a longer period of time.

An example of an effective orientation program that affects student retention is one at Corning Community College (Reimanis 1973). It is based on the premise that many incoming students have unclear values and goals, that it is natural for new students to be apprehensive and anxious about unfamiliar surroundings and experiences, and that the most important program ingredient is exhibiting a genuine faculty and staff interest in and concern for the students and their academic and personal development. The orientation involved such activities as weekly rap sessions, short courses, group as well as individual counseling and advising, and self-concept-oriented encounter groups. Specific activities were targeted to the needs of particular groups, and specially trained faculty were involved.

Illustrating the potential importance of properly designed orientation programs, in the WWISR study orientation programs targeted to reduce student attrition were found to rank third in the amount of action program impact on retention. In addition, the exemplary retention programs highlighted, because of their impact on retention, included several that were primarily orientation programs or combinations of orientation programs.

Policy change. The WWISR study found that 11 colleges and universities (out of almost 1,000 institutions) reported new policies and structures designed and promulgated specifically to improve retention. The average impact on retention of these policies and structures ranked higher than that for any other type of retention program at these 11 institutions. Furthermore, a couple of the exemplary retention programs focused largely on changing the policies, scheduling, regulations, and structure of the institution. These findings suggest that such change may be crucial for really influencing retention. Current organizational structure and policies easily can encumber and deter improvement in retention unless they are formally evaluated in terms of their positive or negative impact on retention. For example, if any current policies constrict or discourage meaningful student-student and student-faculty interaction outside of the classroom, retention rates are affected adversely. Similarly, the research supports the contention by Beal and Noel (1980, p. 13), that institutional policies and procedures should be periodically reviewed "in order to make the college experience as comfortable as possible for students without the unnecessary 'hassle' and encumbrance caused by an insensitized bureaucracy."

Policies of support for the various types and appropriate combinations of action programs already have been implied in the previous section as important for student retention. Other policies and procedures mentioned in the literature that have been documented by experience in particular contexts are listed below:

- Allow students to have a year to hit their stride before becoming eligible for dismissal (Heath et al. 1973).
- Allow juniors to start with a fresh cumulative grade point average so they will not be penalized (Heath et al. 1973).
- Provide promotion and pay increase incentives for faculty development participation (Heath et al. 1973).
- Make it easier for students to come and go (Heath et al. 1973).
- Give credit for life experiences (Heath et al. 1973).
- Have *logical* rules and regulations (Heath et al. 1973).
- Involve *all* segments of the college in retention (Heath et al. 1973).
- Make sure that grading is nonpunitive (Heath et al. 1973).
- Make information and staff available to process late applicants (Heath et al. 1973).
- Make sure that the tuition and fee refund policy does not provide an incentive to be out by a certain day (Michlein 1977).
- Conduct pilot studies of adaptations of programs working elsewhere that seem relevant (Michlein 1977).
- Give credit for successful completion of developmental courses, so that motivation to complete is stronger (Michlein 1977).
- Make retention a top institutional priority (Michelin 1977); for example, appoint a retention committee (with representatives from all segments of the campus) and a formal retention coordinator who reports directly to the president.
- Do not give failing grades for late withdrawals (Vail 1966).

Additional potential policies that, based on synthesis and analysis, can affect retention have been proposed by various authors including: Beal and Noel (1980), Pantages and Creedon (1978), Bradley and Lehmann (1975), Cope and Hannah (1975), Astin (1975c), and Rouche (1967).

Other approaches. A variety of other action approaches that could have promise also were suggested by one or more studies in the literature. They are listed below:

- Nonpaid work education programs (National Association of Secondary School Principals 1973).
- Program to foster good relations with parents, high schools, and the community (Simmons and Maxwell-Simmons 1978).
- Program making widespread use of students as tutors, peer counselors, and/or staff and faculty assistants. (This program is included here because of the benefits that accrue to the students who are doing the tutoring and the counseling, as well as to those on the receiving end (Lenning et al. 1974).
- Program to encourage institution-wide support for retention (Simmons and Maxwell-Simmons 1978).
- Special programs to motivate students (Simmons and Maxwell-Simmons 1978; Lee 1974).
- Increase in the percentage of minorities on the staff where there are a large number of minority students (National Academy of Sciences-National Research Council 1977).
- Special recruitment/retention programs for minorities (Martinez 1978).
- Improvement of administrative climate (Appel et al. 1977).
- Channeling students for greater retention (Huber 1971).
- A referral service to specialized state agencies, such as vocational rehabilitation and the division of family services (West et al. 1975).
- A college educational theater program to educate and motivate potential student dropouts (Ezekiel 1973).
- A work-experience program where students receive pay for working in their major field (DiFede and Edwards 1976).
- A program to influence achievement motivation (Reimanis 1973).
- A program to assist students in handling their finances (Michlein 1977).
- Half-way houses for those students not living at home (Heath et al. 1973).

There are undoubtedly other action approaches to improving retention. Some possibilities that have been effective for other purposes include: gaming and simulation, retreats, student advocacy by outside "actors" such as community educational brokering agencies, campuses ombudsmen for students, changing locations of particular offices and activities, special testing for diagnosis and placement (often this is done by learning centers or counseling centers), involving students in institutional decision making, and values development or clarification.

Multifaceted approaches to improving retention

As the previous discussion has indicated, a large number of single-facet action approaches in various institutional settings have been effective in improving retention. Thus, it seems logical to hypothesize that packaging complementary single-facet approaches would be a better way of improving retention than using a single-facet approach in isolation. While this hypothesis remains largely untested, evidence from the WWISR study, as well as the research literature in general, offers preliminary and mixed results regarding the viability of that hypothesis.

The WWISR study (Beal and Noel 1980) reports that the multifaceted action programs appear to be better than average in their effectiveness in improving retention, according to the retention index developed in that study. Five categories of action programs had mean retention indexes higher—and therefore were more effective in improving retention—than the multifaceted action programs, which had a mean of 3.29. The five categories with higher indexes were: new policies, structures (3.64); learning and academic support (3.45); orientation (3.44); early-warning systems (3.38); and curricular developments (3.33). Nine categories of action programs had lower retention indexes: advising (3.26); career assistance (3.26); counseling (3.22); peer programs (3.22); faculty/staff development (3.20); other (3.00); dropout studies (3.22); cocurricular activities (2.75); and exit interviews (2.67). As mentioned earlier, from a total of 420 action programs for which the retention rating was two or above, 49 were selected as exemplary (had ratings of five). Of the 49, seven are multifaceted action programs, the characteristics of which are reported below.

• Targeted at all freshmen—A semester-long program with: (a) a student-faculty mentor team directing 1 ½-hour weekly sessions; (b) a career week; (c) diagnostic testing; (d) a special ten-hour skills-development seminar.

• Targeted at residential freshmen—Includes: (a) mentor-peer advisor orientation; (b) on-going orientation; (c) advising; (d) financial aid; (e) special classes; (f) counseling by a special guidance counselor; (g) early warning; (h) workshops; (i) student advisors; (j) peer counseling; (k) career planning; (l) exit interviews; (m) a retention officer.

• Targeted at students in lower half of high school class, or below 18 on ACT composite—Includes: (a) two-day workshop period before the fall semester; (b) weekly meetings between groups of 10 to 12 students and peer advisors for the first nine weeks. Focus is on immediate concerns, academic adjustment, and study skills.

• Targeted at marginally qualified entering freshmen—A specialized summer employment and education program consisting of: (a) non-credit courses in basic reading, mathematics, and study skills; (b) employment in a variety of university-based settings; (c) advising; (d) counseling; (e) financial aid; (f) workshops; (g) student advocacy; (h) peer counseling; (i) career planning.

• Targeted at high-risk freshmen in their first semester, either recent high school graduates or adult students—Includes: (a) intensive academic/vocational counseling; (b) tutoring; (c) block programing; (d) performance monitoring; (e) study skills training; (f) personal attention to bureaucratic problems.

• Targeted at all full-time minority students—Includes: (a) special admissions information; (b) special orientation programs; (c) work-skills development program; (d) special tutoring program; (e) special counseling for low academic achievers.

• Targeted at all full- and part-time handicapped students—Includes: (a) special admissions materials and enrollment assistance; (b) special services to improve student-institution fit, such as help with adapting class presentation to accommodate the handicapped, provision of readers, sign interpreters, mobility aids, special devices; (c) special support services to assist in retention.

A number of multifaceted approaches were also reported in the literature. These are outlined below and two are described in somewhat greater detail:

• Leach (1978), Prince George's Community College, targeted at all students—Includes: (a) targeted information-dissemination strategies; (b) delivery strategies for reducing between- and within-term attrition; (c) learning support services.

• Simmons and Maxwell-Simmons (1978), Stevens Institute of Technology, targeted at minority students—Includes: (a) academic support program; (b) information communication improvement; (c) fostering good relations with high schools, parents, and the community; (d) financial aid; (e) sensitive counseling; (f) encouraging institutional support; (g) staff training.

• West et al. (1975), Central Florida Community College, targeted at minority students—Includes: (a) formulation and use of specific objectives for the academic, affective, and student-support domain; (b) special skills courses; (c) intensive counseling; (d) tutorial assistance; (e) special referral service; (f) special teaching emphases and methods in all courses; (g) financial aid; (h) assistance in dealing with the red tape of college procedures and regulations.

• Appel (1977), four Texas community colleges, targeted at developmental students in vocational-technical programs—(a) application of a systems model of individualized instruction where: students "are told in clear nonesoteric language *why* it is important that they master the course content" (p. 20); specific, concrete, and clearly stated behavioral objectives written for each unit of instruction; preassessment of the students' readiness to observe course objectives; individualized learning modules of appropriate length that use special instructional media and provide frequent practice and knowledge of results; criterion-referenced postassessment of students, and courses periodically revised on the basis of student feedback. (b) The Baker Goal Setting Intervention technique—modified Delphi approach to reaching concensus among administrators, faculty, and students —used to reach agreement on institutional goals, then college administrators worked to facilitate the development of general campus climate supportive of accomplishing those goals. (c) Principles of Glasser's reality therapy model and Rotter's social learning model were incorporated into a process of counseling for internality. (d) Extensive administrator, faculty, and counselor training related to the above three student interventions provided.

• Lee (1974), Middlesex Community College, targeted at low-ability students—Two five-week summer sessions prior to regular enrollment that included: (a) skill building courses; (b) exercises and activities to increase motivation, enhance self-concept, and strengthen self-confidence; (c) special counseling to identify individual needs; (d) additional counseling as needed; (e) tutoring; (f) financial assistance.

• Heath et al. (1973), report by Frank Christensen, learning laboratory director at William Rainey Harper College, targeted at all students—(a) Admissions officials plan their program (including informational materials to be distributed) and train their recruiting personnel for retention. (b) Focus of student activities coordinators is on involvement of students who belong to or participate in an organization or group. (c) Counselors and advisors not only oriented towards effectiveness in counseling and advising activities, but serve as resource people for development of retention programs. (d) Financial aid office personnel examine *total* student needs, not just financial needs.

•Reimanis (1973), Corning Community College, various special targeted groups such as undecided students, educational opportunity program students, and high-anxiety nursing students —Includes: (a) short course to develop achievement motivation; (b) weekly rap sessions; (c) locus-of-control counseling; (d) early orientation program; (e) training technical career faculty in affective/confluent education principles; (f) faculty in-service program on how to facilitate student-centered classrooms; (g) group counseling for anxiety reduction; (h) encounter groups for improving self-concept.

• Fishman and Dugan (n.d.), Community College of Philadelphia, targeted at nontraditional students—Cooperative Learning Program, a two-semester program where students obtain: (a) experience in courses from various curricular areas; (b) training in study skills; (c) career information sessions; (d) tutoring; (e) counselors who follow up on each student and offer assistance as needed.

• Macmillan and Kester (1973), 22 community colleges in Northern California, targeted at potential dropouts—Includes: (a) group testing and early warning; (b) orientation; (c) group counseling; (d) individual counseling; (e) student peer counseling; (f) peer tutoring; (g) basic skills courses; (h) college readiness programs.

It will be noted that all the multifaceted strategies found in the literature were from community colleges. However, a number of programs discussed in the WWISR study are from four-year colleges and universities. Furthermore, in a report from Hofstra University, tentative plans had been made for a unified retention program (McDermott 1975) that included the following: (1) development of a retention committee; (2) obtaining top administration commitment and support for the retention program; (3) inservice training seminars for faculty involving points towards promotion or pay increases as incentives; (4) college environment changes; (5) recruitment changes; (6) adding human development seminars, study skills seminars, and vocational choice courses to the curriculum and evaluating the majors offered; (7) dormitory changes; (8) changes in social life; and (9) financial aid. Ten steps to begin implementating the system were proposed: make an open declaration; state objectives; identify the target populations; communicate with faculty; hold frequent meetings with all involved personnel; offer workshops for students; offer workshops for faculty; establish operational guidelines for assistance referral; seek nonprofessional assistance from students and the community; and educate the college community about student development and intervention.

Clearly, many options are open to an institution for developing a special multifaceted retention program. It would appear that various combinations can work well in reducing attrition and that the choice depends largely on local commitment, the local situation, and on what is feasible in terms of monetary cost and staff time and effort. If the commitment to act exists throughout the institution, which may be more difficult to instill at four-year colleges and universities than at two-year colleges, a cost-effective retention system probably can be developed that is especially appropriate for that institution. And as pointed out by the results of the WWISR study, other types of positive benefits for the campus also can be expected in addition to attrition rates.

Conclusion

From the literature describing the correlates of retention—factors that imply fruitful retention strategies—there are a number of findings related to student and institutional characteristics, as well as to student-institution fit. Among student characteristics, academic abilities and high school grades, aspirations and motivations, and finances (both perceived and actual), all seem to have a relatively high correlation with retention. Among the institutional characteristics correlated with retention were the prestige or academic standing of the institution; adequacy of student support services; availability of residence hall accommodations; and the quality of faculty, staff, and student interactions. Regarding the student-institution fit, a number of theories attempt to explain why this factor is so important. These theories emphasize a variety of factors, including moral, social, and academic integration of students with campus life; the responsiveness of the institution to student needs; and how well the institution realizes student expectations and needs.

The chapter on strategies expressly designed to improve retention begins with a short overview of Beal and Noel's "What Works in Student Retention?" (WWISR) study (1980). Following this, the available literature as well as the results of the WWISR study are reviewed to identify important characteristics of single-facet as well as multifaceted retention strategies. Among the single-facet strategies that have received much attention in the literature and that are more frequently encountered on campuses, according to Beal and Noel, are special early-warning and follow-up programs, orientation programs, advising and counseling efforts, and attempts to provide more learning opportunities and academic support for students. Beal and Noel also report that these strategies are among the more successful kinds of retention efforts that have been tried. Other strategies described in the literature as being very important but encountered less frequently in campus retention programs focus on admissions and recruiting; exit interviews; extracurricular activities; faculty, staff and curricular development; financial aid; housing; and policy changes. Another type of action retention strategy combines two or more single-facet approaches. Although multifaceted programs are relatively infrequent in the literature and do not appear to have been used much on campuses, well-designed multifaceted programs clearly can be effective in improving retention.

The literature on improving retention can be bifurcated into a literature that tries to explain why students drop out and one that describes campus action programs and their effects on improving retention. The first category of studies embraces most research that has been conducted to date, and the second represents an emerging type of study.

One observation is that the two kinds of research efforts need to be better integrated: to date they largely have appeared as quite distinct. Research results focusing on the correlates of retention, on the one hand, can help in designing an effective retention program. On the other hand, research focusing on *why* an action program is effective should be more helpful than simply describing the program and stating how the retention rate was effected.

Two other comments also should be made regarding reporting the results of an action retention program. First, many descriptions of action programs do not provide enough detail, particularly regarding the specific content of the program, where it is housed, who it reports to, institutional context (including local customs, expectations, attitudes, personalities, and politics), and process-related details. Such descriptions would be helpful to educators who are considering adapting an action strategy to their own campus. Secondly, researchers who focus on an action strategy might benefit from the principles and techniques utilized in the program evaluation literature, particularly regarding issues such as cost effectiveness.

The research literature does not really address the program's institutional environment. We would agree with Dr. Robert Cope* (who does much consulting on matters of student retention), however, who believes that the success or failure of an action program may very well depend on where the program is housed administratively and to whom the person heading the program reports. The program must gain the support of all segments of the campus if it is to succeed, and its location in the organizational hierarchy can either facilitate or detract from its success.

On some campuses student affairs personnel are respected by the faculty as experts on students, and so it makes good sense to house the program there. On many other campuses, however, student affairs personnel lack such respect, and here, perhaps, the program should be housed with academic affairs personnel if it is to have institution-wide status and acceptance. On the other hand, academic affairs may be insensitive to the need for full involvement of individuals from other campus offices, or may not know how to motivate such persons for effective participation. In such a case, an independent program reporting directly to the

*Robert Cope, 1980: personal communication.

president may be called for to ensure prestige and avoid favoring one area of the campus over another. However, if there is any kind of a confrontation atmosphere between the faculty and the administration, the program could be seen as a "tool of the administration." Where in the organization the action program should be located and who it should report to, thus, depend very much on the local context including who is committed to the idea, relationships and status, skills available, etc. Because it depends so much on the local context, any kind of a general prescriptive recommendation here about program location and coordination is clearly inappropriate. About all that can be suggested is to analyze the complete local situation carefully in terms of probable relative contributions and detractions of the alternatives being considered. Also, it should be kept in mind that there have been failures as well as successes in all 13 types of action programs discussed in chapter three, so the tactics used and how and where the operations are carried out are determining factors.

Each of the single-facet approaches to student retention has potential disadvantages as well as advantages and costs as well as benefits. Similarly, different approaches may meet different student needs related to retention; where one approach may meet the retention needs of a particular student subgroup, other approaches may better meet the retention needs of different student subgroups. Furthermore, devoting some energy and resources to each of several approaches in a combined and coordinated effort may be less costly and more effective than attempting to achieve perfection for a single approach. Therefore, because they also tend to get more of the campus involved (an important factor, as discussed earlier), our recommendation is that multifaceted approaches should be used as feasible in terms of the staff time, expertise, and other resources available. The components of the multifaceted approach and how it should be carried out depend on a careful analysis of many factors, including the needs of different groups of students, faculty and staff attitudes and relationships, available skills, financial resources, and the relative expected costs versus benefits of different combinations of approaches.

Finally, a point made in the beginning of chapter three should be reemphasized. For some students, the best decision is to leave the college. A few students will realize that they are overly frustrated because college really is "not their thing." Others may not yet be ready for college in terms of maturity and self-concept and may need to stop out awhile to acquire external experiences or to think things through before continuing. Still others may have emotional problems that should be resolved before they continue college. Finally, there are students who should transfer to an institution more compatible with them and their needs.

On the other hand, at all institutions, many students leave who should remain, assuming that their experience can be made more meaningful and rewarding to them. Therefore, although colleges and universities need higher retention rates to keep enrollments up during this difficult decade of the '80s what is best for each student should be the primary criterion of action program success. To emphasize this, perhaps the terminology used should be "improved student persistence rates" (from the perspective of students) rather than "improved student retention rates" (from the perspective of the institution). And such a focus also will result in significantly higher retention rates at the same time that the welfare of *all* students is maximized.

Bibliography

The ERIC Clearinghouse on Higher Education abstracts and indexes the current literature on higher education for the National Institute of Education's monthly bibliographic journal *Resources in Education* (RIE). Most of these publications are available through the ERIC Document Reproduction Service (EDRS). Ordering number and price for publications cited in this bibliography that are available from EDRS have been included at the end of each citation. Readers who wish to order a publication should write to the ERIC Document Reproduction Service, P.O. Box 190, Arlington, Virginia 22210. When ordering, please specify the document number. Unless otherwise noted, documents are available in both microfiche (MF) and paper copy (PC).

Aarons, Howell. "An Evaluation of an Individualized Interpersonal and Interdisciplinary Team Approach to Remediation at Mohegan Community College." Ed.D. research project, Nova University, 1975. ED 115 341. MF-$0.98.

Adams, Glenn A. "Preventative Career Counseling—Proving That It Works." *Journal of College Placement* 34 (Spring 1974): 26-33.

Alfert, Elizabeth. "Housing Selection, Need Satisfaction, and Dropout from College." *Psychological Reports* 19 (August 1966): 183-186.

Alfred, Richard L. "A Conceptual Investigation of Student Attrition in the Comprehensive Community College." Paper presented at the annual convention of the American Educational Research Association, Chicago, April 1974.

_____. *Student Attrition: Strategies for Action.* Kansas City, Mo.: Metropolitan Junior College District, October 1973. ED 085 064. MF-$0.98; PC-$10.97.

Anandam, Kamala. *Annual Report for Open College, 1976-77.* Miami: Miami-Dade Community College, 1977. ED 156 272. MF-$0.98.

Appel, Victor H. et al. *Impact of Administrative Climate, Instruction, and Counseling on Control Expectancy, Anxiety and Completion Rate of Post-Secondary Educationally Disadvantaged and Minority Vocational/Technical Students: Final Report.* Austin, Texas: Department of Educational Administration, University of Texas, December 1977. ED 149 801. MF-$0.98; PC-$10.97.

Astin, Alexander W. *Four Critical Years.* San Francisco: Jossey-Bass, 1977.

_____. *Dropouts, Stopouts, and Persisters: A National Profile.* Los Angeles: Laboratory for Research on Higher Education, University of California, 1975(a).

_____. *Financial Aid and Student Persistence.* Higher Education Research Institute (HERI), Research Report No. 75-2. Los Angeles: HERI, 1975(b). ED 112 804. MF-$0.98; PC-$4.55.

—————. *Preventing Students from Dropping Out.* San Francisco: Jossey-Bass, 1975(c).

Barger, Ben, and Hall, Everette. "Personality Patterns and Achievement in College." *Educational and Psychological Measurement* 24 (Summer 1964): 339-346.

Beal, Philip E., and Noel, Lee. *What Works in Student Retention?* Iowa City, Iowa and Boulder, Colo.: American College Testing Program and National Center for Higher Education Management Systems, 1980. ED 180 348. MF-$0.98; PC-$4.55.

Bean, John P. "Dropouts and Turnover: The Synthesis and Test of a Causal Model of Student Retention." *Research in Higher Education* 12 (Issue 2, 1980): 155-187.

Blanchfield, W. C. "College Dropout Identification: A Case Study." *Journal of Experimental Education* 40 (Winter 1971): 1-4.

Bochniarz, Robert M. "An Evaluation of Specific Effects of the Developmental Studies Program on the Academically Disadvantaged at Glendale Community College." Doctoral dissertation, Nova University, January 1978. ED 152 356. MF-$0.98; PC-$4.55.

Bolyard, Cassandra S., and Martin, C. Joseph. "High Risk Freshmen." *Measurement and Evaluation in Guidance* 6 (April 1973): 57-58.

Bradley, Paul A., Jr., and Lehmann, Timothy. *Attrition at a Nontraditional Institution.* Saratoga Springs, N.Y.: Empire State College, 1975. ED 112 739. MF-$0.98; PC-$3.05.

Branch, Marie. *Faculty Development to Meet Minority Group Needs: Recruitment, Retention, and Curriculum Change, 1971-74. Final Report.* Boulder, Colo.: Western Interstate Commission for Higher Education, July 1975. ED 123 982. MF-$0.98; PC-$7.87.

Brigman, S. Leellen, and Stager, Susan F. "An Examination of the Characteristics of Voluntary College Stopouts, Dropouts and Transfers." Paper presented at the annual convention of the American Educational Research Association, Boston, April 1980. HE 012 750.

Bronx Community College. *Attrition and Student Progress at Bronx Community College, September 1970 to August 1974.* Research Report No. BCC-2-75. New York: Bronx Community College, March 1975. ED 107 343. MC-$0.98; PC-$6.05.

Brown, Noah, Jr. "A Descriptive Research Study of a Developmental Plan for Recruitment and Retention of Minority Students." Unpublished dissertation, 1976. ED 146 254.

Brown, Robert D. "Manipulation of the Environmental Press in a College Residence Hall." *Personnel and Guidance Journal* 47 (February 1968): 555-560.

Buckley, Edmund H. "The Development of Language Skills in the Setting of an Interdisciplinary Remedial Program at Santa Rosa Junior College, California." Unpublished doctoral dissertation, Nova University, November 1976. ED 136 865. MF-$0.98; PC-$12.69.

Carman, Robert A. *A Long-Term Study of the Effects of Tutoring in Developmental Mathematics.* Santa Barbara, Calif.: Santa Barbara City College, n.d. ED 112 983. MF-$0.98; PC-$4.55.

Carnegie Council on Policy Studies in Higher Education. *Three Thousand*

Futures: The Next Twenty Years for Higher Education. San Francisco: Jossey-Bass, 1980. ED 183 076. MF-$0.98.

Chapman, David W.; Griffith, John V.; and Johnson, Russell H. *A Checklist for Evaluating College Recruitment Literature.* Ann Arbor, Mich.: Center for Helping Organizations Improve Choice in Education, 1979. (Available from the National Association of College Admissions Counselors, 9933 Lawler Avenue, Suite 500, Skokie, Ill. 60077.)

Chase, Clinton I. "The College Dropout: His High School Prologue." *Bulletin of the National Association of Secondary School Principals* 54 (January 1970): 67-71.

Chickering, Arthur W. *Commuting versus Resident Students.* San Francisco: Jossey-Bass, 1974.

Chickering, Arthur W., and Hannah, William. "The Process of Withdrawal." *Liberal Education* 55 (December 1969): 551-558.

Cope, Robert G., and Hannah, William. *Revolving College Doors: The Causes and Consequences of Dropping Out, Stopping Out, and Transferring.* New York: John Wiley & Sons, 1975.

Council for the Advancement of Small Colleges. *Users Manual for the Student Attrition Module.* Field rev. ed. Washington, D.C.: Council for the Advancement of Small Colleges, 1978. ED 180 270. MF-$0.98.

Cross, K. Patricia. *Accent on Learning: Improving Instruction and Reshaping the Curriculum.* San Francisco: Jossey-Bass, 1976.

Dallas, Gladys E. *Attrition Prevention through Counseling Among Community College Students: NORCAL, Phase III.* Napa College, 1971. ED 075 012. MF-$0.98; PC-$4.55.

Davis, Billy Hampton. "The Community Junior College Experience as Percieved by Students Who Have Withdrawn." Ph.D. dissertation, University of Michigan, 1970.

Demitroff, John F. "Student Persistence." *College and University* 49 (Summer 1974): 553-567.

Demos, George D. "Analysis of College Dropouts: Some Manifest and Covert Reasons." *Personnel and Guidance Journal* 46 (March 1968): 681-684.

DiCesare, Anthony C.; Sedlacek, William E.; and Brooks, Glenwoor C., Jr. "Nonintellective Correlates of Black Student Attrition." *Journal of College Student Personnel* 13 (July 1972): 319-324.

DiFede, Pat, and Edwards, Larcelous, Jr. "Minority Retention: Innovative Programs—The Broward Community College/Broward Manpower Council Work Experience Program." Paper presented at the annual convention of the National Association of Student Personnel Administrators, Dallas, March 1976. ED 138 911. MF-$0.98.

Domino, George, *Interactive Effects of Achievement Orientation and Teaching Style on Academic Achievement.* ACT Research Report No. 39. Iowa City, Iowa: American College Testing Program, 1970. ED 046 356.

Drake University. *Advising-Attrition Effects: A Twelve Month Analysis.* Des Moines, Iowa: Drake University, October 1974. ED 119 603. MF-$0.98; PC-$3.05.

Eckland, Bruce K. "A Source of Error in College Attrition Studies." *Sociology of Education* 38 (Fall 1964): 60-72.

El-Khawas, Elaine H., *Better Information for Student Choice: Report of a National Task Force.* Washington, D.C.: American Association for Higher Education, 1978.

El-Khawas, Elaine H., and Bisconti, Ann S. *Five and Ten Years After College Entry.* ACE Research Report, vol. 9, no. 1. Washington, D.C.: American Council on Education, 1974, ED 098 847. MF-$0.98; PC-$14.79.

Everett, Carol L. *An Analysis of Student Attrition at Penn State.* University Park, Pa.: Office of Planning and Budget, The Pennsylvania State University, August 1979.

Ezekiel, Margaret. "A Way In." *Theatre Design and Technology* 34 (October 1973): 28-33.

Fenstemacher, William P. "College Dropouts: Theories and Research Findings." In *Tomorrow's Imperatives Today*, pp. 185-195. Edited by Robert G. Cope. Seattle: Association for Institutional Research, 1973.

Festinger, Leon. *A Theory of Cognitive Dissonance.* Palo Alto, Calif.: Stanford University Press, 1962.

Fields, Charels R., and LeMay, Morris L. "Student Financial Aid: Effects on Educational Decisions and Academic Achievement." *Journal of College Student Personnel* 14 (September 1973): 425-429.

Fishman, Florence, and Dugan, Margorie. *Alternative Programs and Services for the Non-Traditional Student.* Philadelphia: Community College of Philadelphia, n.d. ED 129 380. MF-$0.98; PC-$3.05.

Flannery, John; Asbury, Charles; Clark, Cynthia; Eubanks, David; Kercheval, Barbara; Lasak, John; McWorter, James; Skellings, Louise; Smith, Douglas; and Sutton, Connie. *Final Report for the Ad Hoc Committee to Study Attrition at Miami-Dade Community College.* Miami: Miami-Dade Community College, 1973. ED 085 052. MF-$0.98; PC-$3.05.

Giltrow, David R., and Duby, Paul B. "Predicting Student Withdrawals in Open Learning Courses." Paper presented at the annual convention of the National Association of Educational Broadcasters, Chicago, October 1976. ED 134 212. MF-$0.98; PC-$3.05.

Green, William D. "After High School, What?" *American Education* (October 1977): 19-22.

Greer, Linda R. "Persistence and Academic Success Among Non-Traditional Age Students at a Junior College." Paper presented at the annual forum of the Association for Institutional Research, Atlanta, May 1980. HE 012 865.

Grites, Thomas J. *Academic Advising: Getting Us Through the Eighties.* AAHE-ERIC/Higher Education Research Report No. 7, Washington, D.C.: American Association for Higher Education, 1979. ED 178 023. MF-$0.98; PC-$6.05.

Groves, Cecil L., and Carroll, Frank T., Jr. *Relationship of Curriculum and Faculty to Student Retention: Seminar Proceedings.* New Orleans: Gulf Regional Interstate Collegiate Consortium, Southern University, May 1973. ED 111 478. MF-$0.98; PC-$6.05.

Haagen, C. Hess. *Venturing Beyond the Campus: Students Who Leave College.* Middletown, Conn.: Wesleyan University Press, 1977.

Hamilton, Jack A.; Wolff, J. M.; and Dayton, C. W. *Safeguarding Your*

Education: A Student Consumer Guide to College and Occupational Education. Palo Alto, Calif.: American Institute for Research, 1976.

Hayden, Mary, et al. *Choice or Chance: Planning for Independent College Marketing and Retention.* St. Paul, Minn.: Northwest Area Foundation, 1976. ED 135 289. MF-$0.98; PC-$9.37.

Heath, Elinor K., et al. *Retention/Attrition: Preventing College Dropouts.* Washington, D.C.: GT-70 Consortium, August 1973. ED 091 013. MF-$0.98; PC-$3.05.

Heist, Paul., ed. *The Creative College Student: An Unmet Challenge.* San Francisco: Jossey-Bass, 1968.

Holland, John L. *Making Vocational Choices: A Theory of Careers.* Englewood Cliffs, N.J.: Prentice-Hall, 1973.

_____. *The Psychology of Vocational Choice: A Theory of Personality Types and Model Environments.* Waltham, Mass.: Blaisdell, 1966.

Huber, William H. "Channeling Students for Greater Retention." *College and University* 47 (Fall 1971): 19-29.

Husband, Robert L. "Significant Others: A New Look at Attrition." Paper presented at a conference of the Association for Innovation in Higher Education, Philadelphia, February 1976. ED 124 056. MF-$0.98; PC-$3.05.

Iffert, Robert E. *Retention and Withdrawal of College Students.* Office of Education Bulletin 1958, no. 1. Washington, D.C.: Government Printing Office, 1957.

Jaffe, A. J., and Adams, Walter. "Academic and Socio-Economic Factors Related to Entrance and Retention at Two- and Four-Year Colleges in the Late 1960's." New York: Bureau of Applied Social Research, Columbia University, 1970. ED 049 679. MF-$0.98; PC-$4.55.

Johansson, Charles B., and Rossmann, Jack E. "Persistence at a Liberal Arts College: A Replicated Five-Year Longitudinal Study." *Journal of Counseling Psychology* 20 (January 1973): 1-9.

Johnson, Russell H., and Chapman, David W. "Involvement in Academic and Social Activities and Its Relationship to Student Persistence—A Study Across Institutional Types." Paper presented at the annual forum of the Association for Institutional Research, Atlanta, April 1980.

Johnston, Archie B. *Length of Residence for a Junior College Degree.* Tallahassee, Fla.: Tallahassee Community College, 1971. ED 056 681. MF-$0.98; PC-$3.05.

Kamens, David. "Effects of College on Student Drop-Out: Final Report." Boston: Center for Applied Social Research, Northeastern University, 1972. ED 068 038. MF-$0.98; PC-$9.37.

Keniston, Kenneth, and Helmreich, R. "An Exploratory Study of Discontent and Potential Dropouts at Yale." Mimeographed, 1965. Cited in Cope and Hannah, 1975.

Kerlinger, Fred N., and Pedazur, E. J. *Multiple Regression in Behavioral Research.* New York: Holt, Rinehart, & Winston, 1973.

Kesselman, Judi R. "The Care and Feeding of Stop-outs." *Change* 8 (May 1976): 13-15.

Kohen, Andrew I., et al. "Factors Affecting Individual Persistence Rates in Undergraduate College Programs." *American Educational Research Journal* 15 (1978): 233-252.

Kowalski, Cash. *The Impact of College on Persisting and Nonpersisting Students.* New York: Philosophical Library, 1977.

Kuznik, Anthony. "Resident Hall Influence on Student Attrition." *Contact* 7 (Winter 1975): 9-12.

Lanning, Wayne, "Factors Related to College Student Persistence and Withdrawal." *NASPA Journal* 16 (February 1977): 34-37.

Leach, Ernest R. "Marketing: A Strategy for Institutional Renewal." Paper presented at the annual convention of the American Association of Community and Junior Colleges, Atlanta, April 1978. ED 156 242. MF-$0.98; PC-$3.05.

Lee, Glenda E. "A Comparative Study of the Persistence and Academic Achievement of 'Project 60' and Regularly Enrolled Students at Middlesex Community College." Bedford, Mass.: Middlesex Community College, 1974. ED 100 481. MF-$0.98; PC-$3.05.

Lenning, Oscar T. "An Exploratory Study of Factors Differentiating Freshmen Educational Growth." Paper presented at the annual meeting of the American College Personnel Association, St. Louis, March 1970(a). ED 039 574(a) MF-$0.98; PC-$4.55.

————. "Student Factors Related to Educational Growth at a Church-Related Liberal Arts College." Paper presented at the annual meeting of the American Educational Research Association, Minneapolis, March 1970(b). ED 039 573(b). MF-$0.98; PC-$4.55.

Lenning, Oscar T.; Beal, Philip E.; and Sauer, Ken. *Retention and Attrition: Evidence for Action and Research.* Boulder, Colo.: National Center for Higher Education Management Systems, 1980. HE 013 131. MF-$0.98; PC-$10.47.

Lenning, Oscar T., and Cooper, Edward M. *Guidebook for Colleges and Universities: Presenting Information to Prospective Students.* Boulder, Colo.: National Center for Higher Education Management Systems, 1978. ED 156 098. MF-$0.98; PC-$7.87.

Lenning, Oscar T.; Munday, Leo A.; Johnson, O. Bernard; VanderWell, Allen R.; and Brue, Eldon J. *Nonintellective Correlates of Grades, Persistence, and Academic Learning in College: The Published Literature Through the Decade of the Sixties.* Monograph 14. Iowa City, Iowa: American College Testing Program, 1974. ED 105 324. MF-$0.98; PC-$20.51.

Lenning, Oscar T., and Nayman, Robbie L., eds. *Expanding the Role of Learning Centers: New Directions for Learning Services.* San Francisco: Jossey-Bass, forthcoming.

Leon, David J. "Chicano College Dropouts and the Educational Opportunity Program: Failure after High School." *High School Behavioral Science* 3 (February 1975): 6-11.

McDermott, Marie. *Towards a Comprehensive Plan to Increase Hofstra's Retention Rate: A Review of the Literature.* Hempstead, N.Y.: Center for the Study of Higher Education, Hofstra University, March 1975. ED 104 274. MC-$0.98; PC-$3.05.

McGuckin, Robert H., and Winkler, Donald R. *University Requirements and Resource Allocation in the Determination of Undergraduate Achievement. Final Report.* Santa Barbara, Calif.: Community and

Organizational Research Institute, University of California at Santa Barbara, August 1974. ED 096 928. MF-$0.98; PC-$7.87.

Macmillan, Thomas F., and Kester, Donald M. "Promises to Keep: NORCAL Impact on Student Attrition." *Community and Junior College Journal* 43 (February 1973): 45-46.

Marchbanks, Janice B. *Recruiting: The Problem of Attrition.* Report of the National Dissemination Project for Post-Secondary Education. Seattle: Washington State Board for Community College Education, Research and Planning Office, 1974. ED 092 187. MF-$0.98; PC-$4.55.

Martin, Fred H. *Student Follow-up 1: Attrition Study.* Harriman, Tenn.: Roane State Community College, 1974. ED 099 087. MF-$0.98; PC-$4.55.

Martinez, Luciano S. *Report on the Ethnic Minority at the University of Utah with a Specific Look at the Health Sciences.* Salt Lake City: Ethnic Minority Student Health Science Center, University of Utah, February 1978. ED 149 940. MF-$0.98; PC-$4.55.

Michlein, Michael G. *Student Attrition in the Wisconsin VTAE System— Phase II: Final Report.* Madison, Wis.: Wisconsin State Board of Vocational, Technical, and Adult Education, June 1977. ED 146 421. MF-$0.98; PC-$17.51.

Montes, Delia, and Ortega, Ludy. "Retention of the Nontraditional Student Through Peer Modeling." Paper presented at the annual convention of the American Personnel and Guidance Association, Chicago, April 1976. ED 130 214. MF-$0.98; PC-$3.05.

Moore, E. Maynard. "Student Attrition in the Open-Door Community College: A Working Hypothesis." *Community College Social Science Quarterly* 6 (Summer 1976): 34-38.

Moore, William, Jr. "Increasing Learning Among Developmental Education Students." In *Improving Educational Outcomes: New Directions for Higher Education.* Edited by Oscar T. Lenning. San Francisco: Jossey-Bass, 1976. pp. 55-71.

Nasatir, David. "A Contextual Analysis of Academic Failure." *School Review* 71 (Fall 1969): 290-298.

National Academy of Sciences-National Research Council. *Retention of Minority Students in Engineering.* Washington, D.C.: National Academy of Sciences; National Research Council 1977. ED 152 467. MF-$0.98; PC-$10.87.

National Association of Secondary School Principals. *School-Supervised Work Education Programs: Curriculum Report.* vol. 3, no. 2. Washington, D.C.: National Association of Secondary School Principals, December 1973. ED 105 142. MF-$0.98; PC-$3.05.

Neely, Renee. "Discriminant Analysis for Prediction of College Graduation." *Educational and Psychological Measurement* 37 (Winter 1977): 965-970.

Nelson, A. Gordon. "College Characteristics Associated with Freshman Attrition." *Personnel and Guidance Journal* 44 (June 1966): 1046-1050.

Newlon, Lorraine L., and Gaither, Gerald H. "Factors Contributing to Attrition: An Analysis of Program Impact on Persistence Patterns." *College and University,* 55 (Spring 1980): 237-251.

New York State Education Department. *New York State Opportunity Programs, 1972-73: SEEK, HEOP, and EOP at Public and Private Postsecondary Institutions.* Albany, N.Y.: New York State Education Department, August 1975. ED 111 918. MF-$0.98; PC-$6.05.

Nickens, John. "Community College Dropout Redefined." *College and University* 51 (Spring 1976): 322-329.

Noel, Lee. "College Student Retention—A Campus-Wide Responsibility." *Journal of the National Association of College Admissions Counselors* 21 (July 1976): 33-36.

O'Brien, William E. "A Study of Student Levels of Satisfaction with Community College and Senior College Instructional Services." Ph.D. dissertation, Northern Illinois University, 1967.

Ohio State-Wide Advisory Committee on Developmental Education. *Results of Assessment Studies of Developmental Education Programs in Ohio.* Report presented at the Fourth Annual Ohio Developmental Education Conference, October 1976. ED 129 366. MF-$0.98; PC-$6.05.

Panos, Robert J., and Astin, Alexander W. "Attrition Among College Students." *American Educational Research Journal* 5 (January 1968): 57-72.

Pantages, Timothy J., and Creedon, Carol F. "Studies of College Attrition: 1950-1975." *Review of Educational Research* 48 (Winter 1978): 49-101.

Papke, David R. "College Venture: Helping the Stop-Out." *Change* 10 (March 1978): 12-13.

Pascarella, Ernest T., and Terenzini, Patrick T. "Predicting Freshman Persistence and Voluntary Dropout Decisions From a Theoretical Model." *Journal of Higher Education* 51 (1980): 60-75.

Pedrini, Bonnie C., and Pedrini, D. T. *Predicting Attrition/Persistence of College Freshmen: Disadvantaged and Regular.* Omaha: University of Nebraska at Omaha, n.d. ED 132 205. MF-$0.98; PC-$3.05.

_____. *The Usefulness of ACT Scores in Predicting Achievement and Attrition Among Disadvantaged and Regular Freshmen: A Survey and Study.* Omaha: University of Nebraska at Omaha, n.d. ED 128 429. MF-$0.98; PC-$14.19.

Pedrini, D. T., and Pedrini, Bonnie C. "Assessment and Prediction of Grade Point and/or Attrition/Persistence for Disadvantaged and Regular College Freshmen." *College Student Journal* 10 (Fall 1976): 260-264.

Peng, Samuel S., and Fetters, William B. "College Student Withdrawal: A Motivational Problem." Paper presented at the annual convention of the American Educational Research Association, New York, April 1977. ED 148 206. MF-$0.98; PC-$4.55.

Pervin, Lawrence A., and Rubin, Donald B. "Student Dissatisfaction with College and the College Dropout: A Transactional Approach." *Journal of Social Psychology* 72 (August 1967): 285-295.

Princeton Cooperative School Program. *A Survey of College Retention and Attrition in the Princeton Cooperative School Program (Upward Bound) 1966-1975.* Princeton, N.J.: Princeton University, March 1977. ED 143 261. MF-$0.98; PC-$9.37.

Reimanis, Gunars. "Student Attrition and Program Effectiveness." Paper presented at the annual forum of the Association of Institutional Research, Vancouver, Canada, May 1973. ED 132 988. MF-$0.98.

Reiser, Robert A., and Sullivan, Howard J. *Reducing the Number of Withdrawals in Personalized System of Instruction Courses.* Tempe, Ariz.: Arizona State University, March 1978. ED 155 983. MF-$0.98.

Rossman, Jack E. "Released Time for Faculty Advising: The Impact Upon Freshmen." *Personnel and Guidance Journal* 47 (December 1968): 358-363.

Rossman, Jack E., and Kirk, Barbara A. "Factors Related to Persistence and Withdrawal Among University Students." *Journal of Counseling Psychology* 17 (January 1970): 56-62.

Rouche, John E. "Let's Get Serious About the High Risk Student." *Community and Junior College Journal* 49 (September 1978): 32-35.

_____. *Research Studies of the Junior College Dropout.* Washington, D.C.: American Association of Junior Colleges, 1967. ED 013 659. MF-$0.98; PC-$3.05.

Rouche, John E., and Mink, Oscar G. "Toward Personhood Development in the Community College." Paper presented at the annual convention of the American Association of Community and Junior Colleges. Seattle, April 1975. ED 114 137. MF-$0.98; PC-$3.05.

Rowell, James R., Jr. *Student Attrition in Higher Education: A Survey of Recent Literature.* Gainesville, Fla.: Florida State University, 1974. ED 100 413. MF-$0.98; PC-$3.05.

Savicki, Victor; Schumer, Harry; and Stanfield, Robert. "Student Role Orientations and College Dropouts." *Journal of Counseling Psychology* 17 (November 1970): 559-566.

Schalock, H. D. "Structuring Process to Improve Student Outcomes." In *Improving Educational Outcomes: New Directions for Higher Education.* Edited by Oscar T. Lenning. San Francisco: Jossey-Bass, 1976. pp. 25-53.

Schmid, John, and Reed, Stanley, R. "Factors in Retention of Residence Hall Freshmen." *Journal of Experimental Education* 35 (Fall 1966): 28-35.

Schotzinger, Kay A.; Buchanan, Jim; and Fahrenback, William F. "Non-Residence Advisors: A Peer Counseling Program for Commuter Students." *NASPA Journal* 13 (Winter 1976): 42-46.

Schulman, Carol H. "Recent Trends in Student Retention." *College and University Bulletin* 28 (May 1976): 3-6.

Selby, James E. "Relationships Existing Among Race, Student Financial Aid, and Persistence in College." *Journal of College Student Personnel* 14 (January 1973): 38-40.

Sexton, Virginia S. "Factors Contributing to Attrition in College Populations: Twenty-Five Years of Research." *Journal of General Psychology* 72 (April 1965): 301-326.

Silver, Jane H. "The Effect of a Self-Development Seminar on Freshman Learning as Measured by Grade Point Averages, Units Completed, and Retention Rate." Ed.D. practicum, Nova University, 1978. ED 152 357. MF-$0.98; PC-$4.55.

Simmons, Ron, and Maxwell-Simmons, Cassandra. *Principles of Success in Programs for Minority Students.* Hoboken, N.J.: Stevens Institute of Technology, 1978. ED 152 917. MF-$0.98; PC-$3.05.

Spady, William G. "Dropouts from Higher Education: Toward an Empirical Model." *Interchange* 2 (1971): 38-62.

————. "Dropouts from Higher Education: An Interdisciplinary Review and Synthesis." *Interchange* 1 (April 1970): 64-85.

Stark, Joan S. *Inside Information: A Handbook for Institutions Interested in Better Information for Student Choice.* Washington, D.C.: American Association for Higher Education, 1978.

Starr, Ann; Betz, Ellen; and Menne, John. "Differences in College Student Satisfaction: Academic Dropouts, Non-Academic Dropouts, and Non-Dropouts." *Journal of Counseling Psychology* 19 (July 1972): 318-322.

Summerskill, John. "Dropouts from College." In *The American College,* edited by Nevitt Sanford. New York: John Wiley and Sons, 1962.

Terenzini, Patrick T.; Lorang, Wendell G., Jr.; and Pascarella, Ernest T. "Predicting Freshmen Persistence and Voluntary Dropout Decisions: A Replication." Paper presented at the annual convention of the American Educational Research Association, Boston, April 1980.

Terenzini, Patrick T., and Pascarella, Ernest, T. "Toward the Validation of Tinto's Model of College Student Attrition: A Review of Recent Studies." *Research in Higher Education* 12 (Issue 3, 1980a): 271-282.

————. "The Influence of a Living-Learning Experience on Selected Freshman Year Educational Outcomes." Paper presented at the annual forum of the Association for Institutional Research, Atlanta, April 1980(b).

Timmons, Frank R. "Freshman Withdrawal from College: A Positive Step Toward Identity Formation? A Follow-up Study." *Journal of Youth and Adolescence* 7 (June 1978): 159-173.

Tinto, Vincent, and Cullen, John. *Dropout in Higher Education: A Review and Theoretical Synthesis of Recent Research.* New York: Teachers College, Columbia University, 1973.

Tinto, Vincent. "Dropout from Higher Education: A Theoretical Synthesis of Recent Research." *Review of Educational Research* 45 (Winter 1975): 89-125. ED 078 802, MF-$0.98; PC-$7.87.

Vail, Evan. *Retention of Students Over a Three-Year Period (Fall Semester 1962, 63, and 64) Under Three Different Drop Policies.* Riverside, Calif.: Riverside City College, 1966. ED 014 286. MF-$0.98; PC-$3.05.

Vest, Thomas J., and Spino, William D. "The Survival Game—Academic Affairs and Student Personnel." Paper presented at the annual convention of the American College Personnel Association, Atlanta, March 1975. ED 112 303. MF-$0.98; PC-$3.05.

Vogt, Dave. *1976-77 Fall to Spring Attrition at UW-Parkside: A Multivariate Approach.* Kenosha, Wis.: University of Wisconsin at Parkside, May 1977. ED 154 666. MF-$0.98.

Walton, Joseph M. "Retention, Role Modeling, and Academic Readiness: A Perspective on the Ethnic Minority Student in Higher Education." *Personnel and Guidance Journal* 58 (October 1979): 124-127.

Wenc, Leonard M. "The Role of Financial Aid in Attrition and Retention." *College Board Review* 104 (Summer 1977): 17-21.

West, Carolyn et al. *Minority Retention in a Community College Program for the Disadvantaged.* Ocala, Fla.: Central Florida Community College, 1975. ED 151 660. MF-$0.98; PC-$3.05.

White, James H. "Individual and Environmental Factors Associated with Freshmen Attrition at a Multi-Campus Community College." Unpublished doctoral dissertation, George Washington University, June 1971. ED 063 919. MF-$0.98; PC-$12.69.

Yuker, Harold E.; Lichtenstein, Pauline; and Witheiler, Paula. *Who Leaves Hofstra for What Reasons?* Research Report No. 102. Hempstead, N.Y.: Center for the Study of Higher Education, Hofstra University, May 1972. ED 065 045. MF-$0.98; PC-$3.05.

AAHE-ERIC Research Reports

Ten monographs in the AAHE-ERIC/Higher Education Research Report series are published each year, available individually or by subscription. Single copies are $3 each for AAHE members, $4 each for non-members. Bulk discounts available on orders of 25 or more copies of a single report. Add 15% postage/handling fee for all orders under $15. Orders under $15 must be prepaid.

Subscription to ten issues (beginning with date of subscription) is $25 for AAHE members, $35 for nonmembers. Order from Publications Department, American Association for Higher Education, One Dupont Circle, Suite 780, Washington, D.C. 20036; 202/293-6440. Write or phone for a complete list of Research Reports and other AAHE publications.

1979 Research Reports

1. Women in Academe: Steps to Greater Equality
   Judith Gappa and Barbara Uehling
2. Old Expectations, New Realities:
   The Academic Profession Revisited
   Carol Herrnstadt Shulman
3. Budgeting in Higher Education
   J. Kent Caruthers and Melvin Orwig
4. The Three "R's" of the Eighties: Reduction,
   Retrenchment, and Reallocation
   Kenneth P. Mortimer and Michael L. Tierney
5. Occupational Programs in Four-Year Colleges:
   Trends and Issues
   Dale F. Campbell and Andrew S. Korim
6. Evaluation and Development of Administrators
   Robert C. Nordvall
7. Academic Advising: Getting Us Through the Eighties
   Thomas J. Grites
8. Professional Evaluation in the Eighties:
   Challenges and Response
   Glenn F. Nyre and Kathryn C. Reilly
9. Adult Baccalaureate Programs
   Marilou Denbo Eldred and Catherine Marienau
10. Survival Through Interdependence: Assessing the Cost and
    Benefits of Interinstitutional Cooperation
    Lewis D. Patterson

1980 Research Reports

1. Federal Influence on Higher Education Curricula
   William V. Mayville
2. Program Evaluation
   Charles E. Feasley
3. Liberal Education in Transition
   Clifton E. Conrad and Jean C. Wyer
4. Adult Development: Implications for Higher Education
   Rita Preszler Weathersby and Jill Mattuck Tarule
5. A Question of Quality: The Higher Education Rating Game
   Judith K. Lawrence and Kenneth C. Green
6. Accreditation: History, Process, and Problems
   Fred F. Harcleroad